YOUR
VIVID
LIFE

YOUR VIVID LIFE

An invitation to live a
radically authentic life

BY SHAYNE TRAVISS

WATKINS
Sharing Wisdom Since 1893

This edition first published in the UK and USA in 2019 by
Watkins, an imprint of Watkins Media Limited
Unit 11, Shepperton House
89–93 Shepperton Road
London
N1 3DF

enquiries@watkinspublishing.com

Design and typography copyright © Watkins Media Limited 2019

Text copyright © Shayne Traviss 2019

1 3 5 7 9 10 8 6 4 2

Designed by Watkins Media Limited

Typeset by JCS Publishing Services Ltd

Printed and bound in the United Kingdom by TJ International Ltd.

A CIP record for this book is available from the British Library

ISBN: 978-1-78678-162-8

www.watkinspublishing.com

CONTENTS

ACKNOWLEDGEMENTS

To my husband Timm, whose unconditional love and support is the kind you hear about in fiction,

To my fur-babies, Mr Anderson and Oliver, my four-legged hearts, who've been next to me (or on my lap) for this entire process,

To my Mother, for the gift of tenacity, resilience and unconditional love,

To my grandmothers, Betty and Dorothy, for their unfathomable grace and the wisdom learned during those special moments only a grandson will know,

To my father, for the gift and freedom of true forgiveness,

To my dear brother Chris, my muse for radical authenticity, gone too soon, forever in our hearts,

To my nieces, Brianna and Mariah, and my nephew Nathan, for the gift of laughter and legacy,

To my Mother and Father in Law, Marilyn and Harry Emberley, for always having my (our) back. And for the kitchen talks filled with love, wisdom and Marilyn's delicious scones (the chocolate-chip ones),

To my dear friend Crystal-Lee Quibell, for picking up the phone (FaceTime), no matter what, to support me on my literary journey (emotions and all),

To Elsii Faria and Kevin Craddock, for providing me the space to heal and grow, either bare-foot in the woods, or bare-soul at the table,

To my Sister in law Amanda Traviss whose strength and motherhood inspire me,

To my wonderful Sister in laws Tammy Emberley and Mischelle Vance, brother in law Brian Vance and My Nieces and Nephews; Mitchell Vance, Hailey Haldane, Molly Vance and Charlie Haldane for the gift of family,

To my step father Dave McKean for foundational support,

To Brenda (Baby Brenda) Legue Bryson, for showering me with so much love and support through one of the most difficult times in my life,

To Eloise Morrison, whose kindness opens my heart,

To Linda Cooper, the queen of grace,

To my American soul sisters Jodi Clauss Salata and Raquel Benavidez, whose laser-sharp intellect and heart wisdom always walk me home,

To T.J. Collina Ashton for drawing the curtains to another world,

To Sharon Quirt for wrapping me (us) in loves arms,

To my step father Dave McKean for foundational support,

To Arielle Ford, for taking my call and showing me the path that led me here,

To my 'fairy godparents' Ed and Deb Shapiro,

To my spiritual Momma Liz Dawn Donahue,

To Jeff Brown, for his grounded guidance,

To Oprah Winfrey and the 'Super Soul' conversations that lifted me higher,

To Elizabeth Gilbert and *Eat Pray Love* for the many days and nights (over 100) snuggled up absorbing your wisdom,

To Don Miguel Ruiz, for writing the words that shifted my world,

To Alan Watts and Osho, for the words that shook it,

To my Good Vibe Tribe and fellow Vivid Life Journeyers, you know who you are,

To every host on VividLife Radio. My days and nights spent producing with you were pivotal,

To the help and wisdom of everyone who contributed to VividLife.me,

To Maranda Pleasant for her kick ass realism and support,

To Blake Bauer, for the introduction to the quintessential publisher,

To 'Your Vivid Life' gate keeper, Etan IIfled (Owner, Watkins Publishing),

To my publisher Jo Lal (Watkins Publishing), for believing in me, refining my message to perfection, and allowing my authentic voice (all of it) to shine through,

To Vicky Hartley (Watkins Publishing), for championing my book globally,

And to everyone on the Watkins Publishing team (Kate Latham, Gail Torr, Ailsa Floyd, Daniel Culver, Lydia Martin, Georgie Hewitt), for bringing this to life and to the world! Everyone and everything on our journey, whether a brief encounter at a cafe, a chance encounter through grief, a schoolmate, a business colleague, a life-long friend, a brother- or sister-in-law, a winding road or a rolling stream contribute to living a Vivid Life, and I'm grateful for them all, because each one has contributed to the wisdom birthed through this book.

We're in this together!

Shayne Traviss

YOUR INVITATION

Are you ready to shut out the noise, take a road trip through your mind, focus on what you want the way you want it, and deliver that in a manner that is straight-forward and fulfilling?

Since I was a little boy I always knew that I was different. That the dream I had for my life didn't look like the options being presented to me. So I chose the road less travelled. I chose a boundless life of adventure, a rollercoaster of epic cosmic dimensions.

From a life of drama, drugs and desserts to chasing an ideal of success that wasn't the healthiest; from working in retail and health food stores to the music industry, television and radio, and fitness and wellness – there was a common thread. From my lemonade-stand desire as a child, then writing, producing and organizing journeys for personal development, it was my personal undertaking to transform my story to create a new one, and to connect and inspire others in doing so. But where the struggle presented itself was in the 'how': how to let go of the story (conditioning), break through the resistance that follows and live a life of clarity, connection and inspiration.

As soon as I was faced with a decision, every school teacher, bully, librarian, friend and parents' voice rose within me as a collective resistance: 'You can't', 'That'll be hard', 'Are you sure?', 'What will people think?', 'You'll be letting us down', 'But, what if you fail?', 'You're not good enough' … You know the voices, right?

They're everyone else's except your own – creating an anxiety and confusion that keeps you stuck and afraid, a deer in headlights. **And, until the pain of remaining the same is worse than the resistance of change, you will remain the same.*** A prisoner of the collective idea as opposed to your own. And until you care enough about yourself and living the life you desire, until you give yourself the space to eliminate distractions, conditioning and get silent enough to listen to your own desires – to listen to the whispers within that are guiding you in the direction of a life that is easeful and fulfilling for you – you will be but a puppet that is picked up and put down as others desire.

Does this resonate with you? Do you have a desire to change? To become more of who you are? To live a radically authentic life? A life that is Open, Connected and Soulful – whether personal, business or social.

I've done it and I'd love to show you how you can too. Join me on a road trip through your mind where I use my own personal stories and insights to guide you in eliminating conditioning, breaking through resistance and helping you gain the clarity you need to live a radically authentic life.

I know, I know … everyone – every guru, politician, religious leader, mom, dad and friend – tells you how to live. Tells you their idea of how to live your life, and I could just be another. However, I know that what works for one doesn't always work for the other. So this book isn't about everyone else. This book isn't even about me. **This book is the possible catalyst to finding out more about you.**

I am not offering up another blanket theology or twelve-step program; what I am offering up is a series of musings designed to show you where you are conditioned, where you are resisting and how to take a closer look around and perhaps uncover a little bit more of yourself and how to live happier, healthier and wealthier amongst the chaos.

---

* Adaptation of an original quote attributed to Tony Robbins

Drama, Drugs and Desserts

This pretty much sums it up for me. My life. From a little boy to a grown-ass man, these three things have had such a profound effect. From outer drama working its way inside then outward again, to a life surrounded by alcoholism and drugs, to tea parties with delicious desserts with my grandmothers and my 'good vibe tribe'. That was it. And man, has it been a ride. Life has been full of opportunities for me to make lemonade from lemons. And I've always seemed to have the know-how – but it doesn't mean I haven't suffered. Every time asking, 'Why me?'

From some of my first experiences rooted in suffering, violence and violation, to growing up with a single mother distracted by financial survival and a heartrending past while doing her best to guide two growing boys, and a father wrestling the demons of his past while unconsciously projecting them through anger, violence and suppression. To struggling through school being super-sensitive, emotionally wounded, radically different than 'the norm' – and ostracized and bullied for it all, by guardians, teachers and peers. Life became an experience in the depths of emotional poverty which I have spent my entire adult life trying to overcome. Trying to find me amongst a life of conditioning.

Imagine that your very first life experiences are rooted in pain and struggle. Ask yourself what that does to you. How as just a wee boy you were conditioned to think that men were something to be feared, that relationships are about conflict and control, and that alcohol, drugs and partying are the way out.

But then there were the tea parties. The ones I had with myself and my imaginary friends in the heart of our home in 'the ghetto' where I definitely snuck some sweet delight, or in the back yard of my grandmother's country home with loads of desserts (and cheese), or with my late grandmother at the opening of our (me and my husband) new retail store in the prettiest part of town with a tower of cupcakes that amazed everyone who attended and laughter that could be heard through the neighbourhood.

Life wasn't all suffering, and oh how grateful I've been for those moments of sweet relief and the heart wisdom (those deepest moments of love, connection and understanding with the world around us) I've learned on the backdrop of carefree and sunny days with earth angels. But where the deepest growth has come has been from the depth of my darkest hours: walking through the high-school halls of what felt like a prison with my head down in hopes that no one would notice me, struggling to find myself, and to be seen in a world that seemed to be against who I was, reaching out for help and protection from those who I now know weren't capable, lying in bed depressed for days, stuffing it all down with food, using drugs and alcohol to escape from it all, and praying to God for the day it would all be over.

'God' played a leading role in my life both in light and in darkness. I was a devout Pentecostal, raising my hands and speaking in tongues for the Lord, then I went to despising its very name as it was used in judgement against me as a gay man wanting to marry the love of my life.

The light and dark. The ebb and flow. This is life – there will be sunny days and there will be storms. But the power is in knowing who you are amongst it all and not lingering in any one place, just staying long enough to find your treasure and realizing that it's within you wherever you're at. But it takes your experiences, your outward journey inward, to undercover it. This is earth school and we are its students. Students of life.

And my hope is that with the best of my ability I use every experience as an opportunity to learn more and more of who I am, to shed the life I've been conditioned to live, to break through the resistance so heavily pushing against me and live a life of clarity, connection and inspiration and then maybe, if you're ready, I am here to shepherd you.

It's not the easiest path, that's for sure. Living a Vivid Life of awareness has its challenges, even when you think it's all over and that the suffering is gone, in comes more. So you go deeper and deeper. Like the layers of an onion, you keep peeling and peeling and eventually you get to the core only to realize it's not a core, that there are more layers and more onions. **And such is life. It keeps showing up. However, we get to choose to be victims or victors, and the greatest achievement of all is to know yourself, to have your feet grounded in the earth and your hands reaching for the sky, and to do your best to integrate that in everything you do.**

We are all an expression of the universe's power to create. So why not create what you want as opposed to allowing yourself to be picked up and put down like a puppet? Stand up. Let go of the story (conditioning) and create anew. Your way.

There was a time long ago when I believed the conditioning, that I was a 'worthless faggot' that only deserved to suffer. That I was an abomination to 'God'. That there was something about me that was so horrible I deserved every beating, tongue lashing and traumatic experience I had ever been through. So much so that at 17 I tried to take my own life and almost succeeded. But there was also something inside of me that was untouched by it all. A big ball of light that had the ability to love even in the darkest moments, even the darkest people. And it was when I woke up in the emergency room – groggy, barefoot, barely clothed and with charcoal on my lips – that I realized I was being given a second chance. And that I was a warrior of the light, fed by darkness but never consumed by it.

Being in the psychiatric hospital was the first step on my path to freedom. It was the day I finally spoke up, told my story and felt it begin to let go.

'The wound is the place where the light enters you.'

Rumi

And the light entered me that day. Every experience that happened to me began to feel like it happened through me. The only way I can describe the experience is that I felt like I was floating, and even though it rained on that day, my entire body, mind and soul was filled with light.

I was beginning to feel what freedom felt like. At least momentarily. And I experience those moments of freedom even today. They come and they go, but what I know now that I didn't know then (well, I know a lot more now than I did then!), one thing I know for sure is that the clearer I am and the more seated I am in the self, then the more full my cup and the less I take it all personally and the more I enjoy the ride.

We are constantly being given the opportunity to become who we are; our outward experiences catalysts to our inner knowing.

Ready, Set, Go

Eleven years ago I left the corporate world, claimed bankruptcy and set out on a journey of self-inquiry from a mini laptop in a wee village east of Toronto, Canada. Without any personal connections, I created VividLife.me, a personal development movement that reached millions around the globe.

From an extremely challenging life – from abuse to bullying, to chasing an ideal of success that wasn't healthy – and with over 20 years of marketing, promoting and producing others, I decided to open a new chapter in my life. I focused my VividLife.me network on my own life experiences, travels and inspirations, and my desire to prompt others to reach out to create their own vivid life.

I've struggled to find myself and my place in the world. Life's challenges can shut some people down, but I channelled my experiences into learning more about myself, undoing conditioning, breaking through the resistance that follows and living a radically authentic life.

This is not another book you're going to breeze through, tell your friends about, maybe Instagram a picture of yourself reading it and then go back to the same life that brought you to it in the first place. This book is a journey through your mind, using my personal experiences and what I've learned as a student of life to shine light on where conditioning and resistance are holding you back and how you can break through it all to live life *your* way. The way you were born to live: radically authentic.

PART I

STOP LOOKING OUTSIDE FOR WHAT'S INSIDE – UNDOING CONDITIONING

Do you feel like you're unconsciously being pulled around by conditioning and distractions, and are beyond ready to drown out the noise so your heart and soul are once again the leaders?

Lifting our heads, looking around a little and stepping away from all the noise can really show us the deep-rooted conditioning and consistent resistance we have to living the life we want, as opposed to the one that we've been conditioned to live. Even now I still question myself and my path. I battle with my head (conditioning) and my heart (inner knowing). But what I know for sure is ... that every time I follow my heart I end up exactly where I am supposed to. Every experience might not have been sunshine and rainbows but it's what I needed to gain a greater understanding. How many times on your path have you got the call – first it was whispers, then screams, but you resisted?

I've been there, many times, and I'm sure I'll be there again. However, every time I trusted my heart, put conditioning in its place and mustered up the courage to break through resistance, I at first felt freedom, then some sadness set in. But I gave it its space. As my dear friend Deb Shapiro (mindfulness and meditation teacher and author) says, 'Invite it in for a cup of tea,' and I did. I moved through the very thoughts and emotions many of you have experienced and are experiencing now, but a little differently than I ever had before. I had a cup of tea with them. I allowed them to come, to move through me, to teach me and then to let go of me so that I could step on this new path with connection, clarity and inspiration. More suffering came and I let it in, and so happiness and joy came as well. I let them in too. And what I truly began to realize was that what caused most of my suffering was the inner conditioning that I had allowed to define me. My mind took me back to that age-old question every parent, teacher, aunt, uncle and friend asks, 'What do you want to be when you grow up?' 'Fireman, doctor, lawyer, teacher …?' I didn't know then and I still don't have the answer now. But what I do know is that I want to be doing what I love, where I love, the way I love with who I love, and as I grow and evolve so do the people, places and experiences that surround me. So what feels like the right path for me is always changing and that's ok. What's most important is that it's mine.

Our entire lives are conditioned from the time we are born, in the clothes we wear, the toys we play with, our religion, education and social class, and even the career we will have and where we will live. Our parents, grandparents, aunts, uncles, teachers and religious leaders program us to fulfill the lives they believe we should live, without ever giving thought to the fact that we're born an individual with our very own desires and destinies to fulfill.

But it's not their fault, they were conditioned too. And blame will leave us stuck victims, never taking accountability for ourselves, our own awareness and growth. But where did it all begin? How can we undo what's been done? Perhaps we aren't even aware that we're conditioned? Maybe we haven't given ourselves the time or space to be aware?

Behind all the stories we tell ourselves and the conditioning and beliefs we've adopted, there is a voice that is constantly whispering our truth, an internal GPS that knows our 'yes's and 'no's, our 'this way's or 'that way's, our core intent. And if we stay there long enough and if we listen to its guidance, we will find that it's always drawing us closer to our own voice, a life on our terms free from conditioning and the beliefs and opinions of others, where we know our own strength, our own beauty. We see our golden wings and we realize that our conditioned selves are deceptive and, with our new-found wisdom, we take flight. Not without a little, or perhaps a lot of turbulence, but with the self-awareness to ride with it and not against it.

Are you ready to shine awareness on your conditioning – taking inventory of where you are, what got you here and learning how you can keep conditioning in check?

Great. Then here we go!

CHAPTER I

BE STILL AND KNOW – SOLITUDE

It all starts the moment we begin to wake up. We reach out, perhaps with our eyes still closed, for our phones. We open our eyes, the bright light temporarily blinding us, and while we wait for our eyes to adjust, we open Facebook – and the distraction from ourselves begins.

Perhaps we read the latest news, usually doom and gloom, or see that our friends seem to be living epic lives travelling around the world, eating at the best restaurants, watching sunrises in Iceland and sunsets in Bali while we're pulling the comforter a little tighter on a cold winter's day.

Articles fly by entitled '3 Steps to a Better Life', 'Life Hacks for the Family on The Go', 'How to Lose 30 Pounds in 30 Days' or '10 Ways to Attract Your Soulmate'. You know the ones, right?

Wow! It's like you've been hit by a truck containing all the doom that life has to offer and all the potential solutions all at the same time. Your head is full of mental chatter and you haven't even got out of bed yet.

But that was your choice, yes? As soon as you had one eye open you grabbed for your phone. No one passed it to you. There wasn't some uncontrollable force within or outside of you who forced you to pick it up, read through every grueling headline, or fill yourself with so much information about how other people live better lives, spend more time with family, lose weight or attract their perfect partner, right? It was you.

It would seem that for some reason you – we – are all at times afraid of being alone with ourselves. We've grown up in a world that is so infected with distraction that to stop and listen to the sound of our own inner voice is alien to us. We've filled our heads with so much of what others think that we don't even have a clue what we think.

Go ahead – give it a try right now. Ask yourself what you are really thinking, and I guarantee you a whole lot of distraction and other people's ideologies will fill your head. And perhaps you will start to get frustrated and uncomfortable – your chest will tighten and your head will start to feel heavy, because amongst all the chatter and the conditioned thoughts in this state, you just can't seem to grasp what's yours.

And if I asked you to take just 15 to 20 minutes right now to be alone with yourself, a similar reaction would occur – only this time your head would fill with all the reasons you don't have time. 'I have to get ready for work', 'I have to make breakfast for the kids', 'put in the laundry', 'clean up the dishes', 'finish a paper', 'answer emails'. The to-do list just goes on and on in the aimless pursuit of filling our days with stuff so that we don't have to be alone with ourselves, and our thoughts.

'Cause that's scary, right? I know. I can barely breathe sitting here thinking about it, wondering what's going to come up. Maybe the fact that you're living a life that you don't want in the hope of buying the freedom to live it later – working a lucrative career that doesn't make you happy. And that's too painful. We don't want to look at that. Or maybe you've been avoiding a necessary conversation with a friend about the way they are treating you for fear of rocking the boat, or avoiding fully examining your life for fear of seeing the reality that is your life versus the distractions you're defining yourself by.

Whatever it is, as soon as we think about being alone it all comes flooding in. We've become afraid of solitude, for fear of not wanting to actually look at ourselves or that we'll be judged as lazy for sitting there and doing nothing.

Solitude at some point seems to have gotten a bad reputation. **And how can we truly know ourself unless we get still enough to listen to just ourself? Unless we give ourself the time and space to tune in.** Perhaps we should change the name to 'Me Time' or better yet – 'Finding Me Time'. Does that feel better? Will that work now?

No matter what we choose to call it, solitude is necessary for our development. Without taking the time to 'be still and know' ourself, we are just a distracted individual sifting through the noise of other people's thoughts, ideas and ideologies; the noise of the life we let happen around us, never being able to identify our own self and our own choices. Our lives become dictators of the collective as opposed to a democracy of our own free will.

Solitude holds the key to the freedom of our own awareness – the time and space where we get to check in with ourselves, to find our own truth and to speak that into the world with all we've got. To reverse the outside-dictates-inside world we've been conditioned to live, and start living our inside outside instead.

Giving our true selves to the world gives others permission to do the same. Our outside world has become a world that's out of touch, where our stories, pictures and posts have far more value than the actual events it took to collect them. Do you miss the sunset because you're worrying over the shot? Does your child's funny comment mean more because of how it sounds later online rather than in your heart?

Finding Your Own Solitude

So, what is solitude anyway, and what does it mean to you? What do you think of when you think of solitude? Do you see yourself all alone in a quiet padded room, or sitting alone by a brook? Are there other people in sight, or are you a long way from anyone? What are you choosing to do?

Wikipedia describes solitude as 'the state or situation of being alone'. So in that case, the time, space or modality doesn't really matter much, right? As long as you're alone. Remember that it's not as simple as being away from everyone else. We're very good at not being truly alone – we're usually on our phones, listening to music or a podcast, or distracting ourselves from being in our own heads. Let's think of solitude as taking time to be with our own true self, and feeling ok about that.

And when you are, when you give yourself permission to take the time, to find a space to be alone with just you and your thoughts there is so much there to discover. Alone, without distractions, witnessing yourself, your thoughts and emotions, your inner search with practice brings clarity, freedom and self-renewal.

And the cool thing is that you get to decide how you do it – when, where and how. So how do you like your solitude? With a cup of tea and a warm blanket, a nature walk on a crisp fall day, or – for the OCD in you – in a pristine room all dressed up with your Yoga mat, your crystals and your eye pillow? Now you're ready.

There are so many ways in which we can practice solitude and not one of them is the right or wrong way. Today you may choose a walk and tomorrow to sit still on a pillow. The right way is whatever way feels most authentic to you. So make sure you check in with yourself before your practice. What I know for sure though is that every time I tried to force myself to do something that I wasn't naturally drawn to, I suffered.

I remember the first time I was introduced to Meditation. I was super-excited because from what I had heard and researched this was the key to my peace of mind. Picture it, I showed up to a class with my brand new green Yoga mat (green represents the heart chakra) in my Thai fisherman pants and tank top and I sat down with my legs in perfect position (I looked up how online …) I put my hands in the lotus position, closed my eyes and started listening to the instructor.

But my heart started racing, my thoughts were out of control, and of course I found myself thinking more about whether I was doing it correctly or not than letting myself relax and slip into the peace of mind I was promised.

I tried over and over again because I was determined to make it work. Just like most of my childhood and adult life, I was trying to follow the path I was told to take versus getting still enough to listen to my own heart. Does this sound familiar?

Anyway, I'm sure Meditation in its 'proper' form works for some but it just didn't work for me, and so as soon as I allowed myself the space to be a rebel about it, I found the way that worked for me. And I do that, perhaps not every day, but I go when I feel within me that I need it the most.

There is a form of solitude prevalent in many religions and spiritual traditions around the world. It's crucial for our mental and spiritual development, and our awareness. And because our world has become so culturally intermingled we have a smorgasbord of options to choose from. We can pick just one or we can dabble in them all. That's the power of authentic awareness. You get to play the creator every day in every way.

My Story: Into the Woods

It was a warm summer's day and, as I woke up, my head was already pounding. The sound of construction just outside the window and the debris and dust it tossed around was filling my sinuses and I just wanted to take off my shoes, drive up the road and run barefoot through the forest.

Shinrin Yoku in Japanese, or Forest Therapy in English, is a trend that is really starting to catch on, but I find this strange: that we have to make it a thing in order for people to do what was once very natural and common.

It's sad that we have become so disconnected from our natural element. I believe, pun intended, that it's the root of much of our suffering, this disconnection from nature and essentially from those around us.

We're so wrapped up in doing, having and showing that we've forgotten about just being. Connecting.

I'm totally guilty of it too; however, I have a constant awareness tugging at me and reminding me that nature is where I find solace, where I connect and regenerate and heal.

Taking off my shoes and feeling the dirt beneath my feet, looking up through the cedars, watching light dance through the leaves is where I regularly need to be. Magical and transformational even if just for a moment, it fills me up. Pictures flash through my mind of times at The Hive Centre, a wonderful holistic health community just up the road from my home, running barefoot through the paths and dipping my feet in the brisk spring-fed brook, collecting rocks and picking watercress. Divine.

Last weekend I attended a retreat there titled 'Naturally Gifted – Relax, Reflect and Create', led by my dear friends and co-owners of The Hive Centre, Elsii and Kevin. Elsii is an award-winning artist, wild food expert and wonderful human being and Kevin is a musician and expert navigator always steering us back on path when we get lost in the forest. I often refer to them as *familia* (Portuguese for family) as Elsii is Portuguese.

I arrived precisely in time for lunch with my friend, Brenda. For those of you who know me you know how much I love a good meal. I had missed the morning Frequency Meditation as I was strolling the beach with my puppies (they're actually 11 and 12) – Mr Anderson and Oliver, as I wouldn't see them for the rest of the day.

Lunch is a favourite thing of mine at The Hive Centre, especially when Elsii makes it; it is always something notorious, delicious and educational. Elsii likes to throw things in she's collected from her walks in the forest, edible wild food.

It was so nice to meet everyone who attended. Some of whom I've been friends with on Facebook but had never really connected in person. How divine is it to connect in person? Such a difference, face to face, story to story, hug to hug … it wakes up your soul.

After lunch we took a long walk along the country roads and in the forest collecting plants, flowers and anything else we may have found with which to create works of art. I did it all barefoot of course, with a little apprehension because it had been a while. I was so happy that I did though, it was pure bliss.

In this place there was no past, no future, just pure presence. There were others around, but I felt alone and strong, focused on my task and in tune with nature. My body tingled with connection deeply rooted in the earth. My heart was open. I listened to the trees, the sound of the water rolling over the rocks, the leaves scrunching under my feet, mud between my toes and the sweet sounds of laughter amongst the group as we ventured through the forest. Home sweet home.

When we returned from the forest with our collection of wild things there was a silence, and a peace, as we all went to work creatively using what we had collected to express the intentions we had set earlier. My intention was wealth, in all aspects of my life. And after my natural masterpiece was complete I took in a few breaths, looked at what I had created and asked the universe, 'What is this saying to me?'

***

And what it said to me was 'slow, steady, connected, focused'. And I felt that, right in the root chakra. That place that was a little shaky and filled with uncertainty from a life of hardship and conditioning. I – we all – have been conditioned to be faster and do more and work harder, whatever it is we need to do in order to 'bring home the bacon'. I really hate that phrase. I don't eat pork, but it's what came to me. And it had been ten years since I left my corporate job in search of what fills me up; however, there is still some clearing to do there. We're all a work-in-progress – students of life, right?

What I learned from that retreat, and what I am constantly learning, is the ebb and flow of life. **That life is a series of**

experiences that are ever so gently showing up to remind us who we are and what we need to walk us home. Whether it's the gentle voice of the forest calling us to connect, or the pounding headache reminding us that we've been too hard on ourselves.

Your heart, your body, your soul – they know. They are the constant forces ever so gently, and sometimes not so gently, leading us in the direction of our highest good. Whatever that might be only we know, and only if we get still enough to listen.

I'm ever so grateful for the whispers, and the screams, and for people like Elsii and Kevin who provide others with the space to connect and heal.

The Practice of Solitude

'Oh Jeez,' as my husband would say. The Practice of Solitude. I'm triggered already, my breath is shortening and the resistance is kicking up in me like a hurricane. But why? It's just a word, right? But words have meaning to us: attachments, stories, beliefs. And our beliefs create our realities and, left unquestioned, unexamined, they can cause a great deal of suffering.

My first belief – about the word practice – is that it means pain. It means practicing things that I don't want to do to be part of some team which I never wanted to be part of in the first place, but I long to be part of something so I settled. I did push ups, chin ups, shuttle runs, none of it any fun, none of it what I wanted to do. I would rather have been having tea with my grandmother, but she wasn't a ten-year-old boy and I so longed to connect with someone my own age, my own gender. But it seemed they weren't into practicing how to throw a proper English Tea, but to kicking around balls and getting dirty. So the word practice meant something very different to me. It meant doing something I didn't want to do for a goal I wasn't interested in – just to 'fit in', and to try to connect with other boys, to be a part of something.

And solitude, well, that's another story. I spent days in solitude, or solitary confinement as you could call it, as a child, from sitting alone in the window of our childhood home in 'the ghetto', to being a loner and walking home from school without any friends.

So neither the word Practice nor Solitude meant good things to me. But like all things, my intrinsic self mustered up the courage to break through my own beliefs and take another look around, to experience them from a different perspective with a new awareness. After all, I'm not a child anymore, right? I've grown from these experiences, not having to follow the leader or being restricted by someone against my will.

I'm free to make my own decisions, to figure out what works for me. And it doesn't have to be what everyone else is doing, or what I've been told. And this Solitude thing, this Practice of Solitude, has some pretty solid history to back it up as a means of direct transportation to our deepest desire, our purest intent, our destiny!

I like the sound of that, destiny! How about you? Don't you want to cut out all the aimless chatter that whips you around in every direction, that picks you up and puts you down like a puppet, that causes you to question yourself even when you know with all your heart and soul what's right for you? Don't you want to silence the drunken monkey that seems to have taken control of your mind and run amok, got it all so chaotic you find it hard to even choose what you're going to have for breakfast 'cause some health guru's nattering in the back of your mind telling you that if you continue to eat eggs you're going to have a heart attack and die. Geesh!

Stop, be still for a moment, drop your shoulders, close your eyes and take a long deep breath. Now let it out. Ah there we go. Now perhaps you're ready to talk a bit about the Practice of Solitude: its history, how each practice has helped others to become clearer and more at peace with themselves and can help you too.

There are as many ways and names for the Practice of Solitude as there are languages. And thanks to globalization we have the opportunity to experience them all and to choose the one(s) that work best for us. In India they meditate, in the Amazon they use Ayahuasca, in Norway they practice Friluftsliv which in English means 'free air life', and in Japan, Shinrin Yoku is 'forest bathing'. Some in the Jewish faith practice Hitbodedut, in Islam they have Muraqaba to watch over one's soul or Tafakkur to meditate over your sins, your environment and the lessons which the creator has created for you. In Mongolia there is Vipassana, 'to see things as they are' and Indigenous Americans use Vision Quest.

When presented with so many options we can become confused, like a deer in headlights, and most often choose the one that's 'trending', whether it actually works for us or not, causing us more mind chatter and taking us further away from our true or authentic self. In order to choose which path or practice of solitude works for us we must give ourselves the time and space to 'be still and know' and then walk in the direction that screams our name.

It's time to step away from the noise and get to know ourselves better, to become more aware. The more time we spend getting to know ourselves the more we understand our purpose here and how that fits in with the whole.

Let's start with a wee tour of some Solitude practices from around the world:

Meditation
Meditation is an ancient mind and body practice which has many forms and techniques all developed to help us focus and witness our thoughts without judgement. It has its roots in the East, India to be specific, where it has been practiced for thousands of years. Most recently it has become somewhat of a phenomenon in the West where, like everything, we have ripped it from its roots, studied it to death and are now developing our own East-meets-West practices which range

from using it in Yoga classes to developing strategic lineages to help Wall Street executives become better at their jobs.

Like everything, as it expands, as we expand, so does the practice and so we get to choose which Meditation works best for us. I have tried everything from Kundalini Meditation and HRM (Heart Rhythm Meditation) to Guided Visualization, and what seems to work for me is, well, different practices at different times, as I and we are always changing and evolving and so do our practices. When I started meditating it made it easier for me to use Guided Meditations as they were really accessible, with thousands being available at our fingertips on YouTube. As I progressed I began to try more advanced types of Meditation, deeply studying each practice in my Yoga teacher training program.

To date, Meditation is not my favourite form of Solitude but its deep scientific and field evidence account for its power to change our brain chemistry and assist in hardwiring our brains for a deeper, more peaceful life.

Friluftsliv

Friluftsliv is a practice in Norway which was first termed in 1859 by the famous Norwegian writer, dramatist and poet, Henrik Ibsen. It is the practice of connecting with presence to your natural environment (nature). To be completely engulfed in nature and whatever you are doing or experiencing while immersed in it. It kind of reminds me of being a kid, filled with excitement and all dressed up like the Stay Puft marshmallow man marching outside at my grandmother's house in the woods, making snow angels without a care in the world. Hours would go by as my cousins and I filled the forest with angels. No matter what the temperature, it seems the more present we were the less we felt the cold. The forest, the snow, the cold, we all became one; like we connected to a place where time didn't exist, and perhaps we did.

But the purpose of Friluftsliv is not to go into nature to do a particular activity or with purpose but just to be in nature, be present to what is and connect to the natural biological rhythm of life. There is evidence to suggest that when we are in nature, in this state, we are deeply connected to the natural rhythm of our brain and circulatory system which creates lasting health effects and evokes a deep sense of lasting inner peace.

Shinrin Yoku

Similar to the Norwegians' Friluftsliv, the Japanese practice of Shinrin Yoku, Forest Therapy or Forest Bathing was developed around the 1980s as a preventative to mental and physical health issues. Sounds odd, eh? We've become so disconnected from our natural environment and engaged with our fast-paced electronic environment that we have to give emo name(s) to rituals or practices that were once second nature.

But whatever we have to call something to entice people back to what's natural, I'm in. Especially when the benefits are reduced stress levels, lower blood pressure and heart rate, increased mental clarity, reduced chronic fatigue, improved mood, and research has even shown it to increase the cells in our body known to prevent cancer and boost our immune system.

No wonder I feel like a million bucks every time I get barefoot and walk the trails at The Hive Centre, one of my favourite places to practice Shinrin Yoku. I actually feel high and the benefits last for days, even up to a week.

The details are in the name 'Forest Bathing'. Google or GPS search for a green space in your area, or if you're lucky enough to have some in your own back yard, or have good friends that live on a nature reserve like me, just take off your shoes if you're risky like that, walk into nature and explore, dip your feet in the natural spring or pond, hug a tree or just lay down and breathe in the fresh air.

I guarantee it will lift you higher while grounding you at the same time. For those brave enough to bare their soles, my dear friend Sue Kenney, who's walked the entire Camino de Santiago and who at one time I thought was crazy, has written a very comprehensive guide on barefooting and the health and wellness benefits – from better sleep to improved glucose regulation and increased immunity. Her book is titled *How to Wear Bare Feet* and available on her website and via Amazon.

Vipassana

Vipassana, meaning 'insight', is one of the most ancient meditation techniques, discovered by Buddha more than 2,500 years ago. Its purpose is to gradually eliminate mental distractions and impulses, eventually leading to a clear understanding and deeper connection to our truth beyond illusions.

It's practiced by sitting still and slowly bringing our awareness to observing both our mind and body, and noticing what we notice without judgement. Not trying to rationalize with the ego mind but sitting still and resting into the deeper awareness behind the ego mind and then eventually with time and practice bringing that full awareness into our lives.

I studied and practiced Vipassana both in my Yoga teacher training program and in several workshops that I have attended throughout North America. It takes great self-control to focus our mind on what's actually happening versus following our conditioned thoughts to conclusions which are illusions. The more we practice this awareness without judgement and break through our conditioned illusionary selves the deeper our sense of self, awareness of our own reality versus the collective or dictated reality, and the more at peace we are with whatever is happening in our mind and body.

With regular practice of Vipassana people have been known to be free from both mental and physical afflictions, discovering the deeper awareness that our thoughts affect our reality both in mind and body.

Reflection: Are You Ready to Step Away?

Solitude and structured practices of solitude have been used to help us maintain clarity and peace of mind for thousands of years. And it seems now, more than ever, we're in desperate need of that peace. We are increasing the speed of living at a rate which is far too fast for us to keep up with. Our lives have become like rockets, under a lot of pressure and ready to lift off into space. So, what we need more than ever is to connect and ground ourselves. **It's amazing what insight comes when we stop long enough to listen and how fulfilled our path becomes when we use what we've found to live authentically.**

Each practice has the same intent, with different yet similar paths, and you get to choose which path feels best to you. That's what it's all about. All are practices of processing, inquiring and connecting to our deeper selves. What's been formally called Shinrin Yoku or Forest Therapy is what helps me to be still long enough to drown out the noise and puts me in touch with myself, my deepest intent and desires and leads me to the wisdom I need to step into my destiny. In order to find a path of your own you have to say goodbye to the path that you've been conditioned to take and choose a path of your own, and to be mindful not to become distracted by your desire to change others rather than to know your own truth, and to give it to yourself and to the world with all you've got. Be aware enough not to fall back into the conditioned life versus having the courage to step into your own.

By not practicing solitude we are constantly running away from ourselves and accepting a state of collective slavery versus a life of our own meaning, truth and radical authenticity. Having the courage to 'be still and know', to take the time to face our thoughts, and to sort out our own from the collective and then acting with conviction from that space, creates a ripple effect giving others permission to do the same.

Solitude can be scary. It causes us to question everything we have ever been conditioned to think, causes us to feel isolated, ostracized from the crowd and even from those we love, and it can create a deep sense of anxiety. But stay with it – close your eyes, take a deep breath and allow yourself to go deeper. In that space you will realize it's better to live a life of your own free will than it is to remain a prisoner of the collective, never allowing yourself to reach the fullness of your potential.

To face our truest selves and to realize our destiny can be overwhelming, because once we realize it we can't take it back and we must summon our courage to break away from our conditioned self and walk our unique path. If it doesn't work, get up and try it again tomorrow. Just do yourself a favour. Don't give up on finding you.

CHAPTER 2

SLOW, STEADY, CONNECTED, FOCUSED

Awareness, or an 'AHA moment' as I like to call it, is the moment when our mind understands what our heart has been trying to communicate all along. Our hearts being our connection to our inner voice or soul, to our greater purpose or intent in this life.

Every day in every way we are gently, and sometimes not so gently, being guided in the direction of our inherent truth. Every experience is walking us home to ourselves. From the subtle voice that whispers 'No – this way,' to the inner scream that creates an awareness in us so immense it can't be ignored. We must use our solitude to kindle this awareness, listen to learn our true self.

And it's up to us whether we pay attention. Sometimes paying attention can be scary. Being aware of our innermost desires can send us on a path that is contrary to what we had planned. It can walk us in the direction of separating from a spouse or leaving a career or perhaps travelling to a place that terrifies us. And our 'rational mind' might not be able to figure out where it's leading us.

Perhaps we might think we've gone mad. Because to follow that voice within us seems to be to step out of the crowd mentality, the conditioning, which we tend to view as making us vulnerable, as putting us in a place to receive criticism. And we all want to be accepted, right? We want to be seen, but perhaps not at the risk of being ostracized for being different.

However, those of us who garner the courage to follow our inner voice of awareness dare to step onto the path that will lead us on an epic adventure, and eventually lead us home to ourselves. It might not look like a safe desk job with a pension, but what can be guaranteed is that if we follow the light of our own awareness through our experiences, joy and pain, emotions and loneliness, we will arrive at the end with an understanding of who we really are and what this journey is all about.

As a young man I remember subtle moments of awareness which came mostly when I was on my own, when I looked back in contemplation on my day and my responses throughout. I remember one time as a tween – I think that's what they call it, I was around 11 or 12 years old – when I had suddenly become afraid of going outside to play with my friends. My monkey mind was running amok again, going over all the reasons that none of my friends wanted anything to do with me, and as I looked out of the window a momentary awareness came to me that inspired a poem, one that I titled 'The Vase', because that was what was next to me on the window ledge as I looked out in sadness at my friends playing on our street.

The awareness that arose from this spontaneous desire to write what I was feeling gave me a deeper understanding of myself and what was blocking me from communicating with my inner self and awareness. It seems this battle between our true spiritual or soul awareness and the 'monkey mind' is intrinsic because I don't remember a time when the two weren't battling it out within. However, it seems that I was born with an innate ability to call it out. Both within my own conflicted thoughts and with others. It didn't always make me popular, but it made me, me.

The times in my life that I've disconnected from and ignored that awareness have been the most turbulent, both internally and externally, and the more I resisted that awareness the louder it got. More experiences would show up, more people. These were both carrying with them an opportunity to see myself, my real self, and then garner the courage to live that out loud in the world.

But I wasn't ready. I wanted to belong. I wanted to listen to my parents, to my church, to my teachers, to my friends. And I wanted so deeply to believe that they had the answers I was looking for. So much so that whenever I was alone with myself I couldn't bear it. The whispers turned to screams and my inner conflict made its way out.

It was like a great drama playing itself out so that amongst it I would wake up and understand what it was all trying to show me, who it was trying to show me. Every experience, every relationship was a mirror shining back at me the light of my own awareness; however, I guess I wasn't ready to look. Perhaps I was afraid to look.

But maybe life is just that – life, a drama unfolding before our eyes, not to us but for us. So that perhaps, one day when we're ready, we can take the time to find awareness, maybe through solitude, self-inquiry, journaling, reading, education, conversation, or, my personal favourite, movies.

Believe it or not, movies have been a key tool of self-awareness for me. The ones that strike a chord I watch over and over again, rewinding (when there were VHS tapes) to parts that spoke to me, to what I now know were leading to my own awareness. To an understanding that surpassed what I'd been taught, or what I'd learned, but something that seemed to have been born within me and that was a constant force in attempting to nudge me in the direction of what was within all along.

Do you feel that pull? Hear that voice? Perhaps right out of a meditation you get a huge AHA moment, or when reading a book something basically jumps off the page or fills you with so much excitement. Sometimes through a conversation with friends or perhaps just a walk in nature all of a sudden some deep sense of awareness downloads out of what seems to be nowhere and gives you the answers you need. And you are able to deal with whatever's been troubling you, or a perspective on a friend or family member that helps you see them with more compassion, or the perfect idea for your next venture. **Awareness is like electricity to our soul. It sets our neurons ablaze with the conviction of our integral being.**

My Story: Snails on the Sidewalk

It was a day like any day. The sun was shining, the birds chirping (very Snow White and the Seven Dwarfs), with the sound of construction off in the distance as I glanced out of my balcony window drinking my morning coffee. I often wake before everyone else and like to sit quietly by myself, often reading.

I begin to hear the sounds of pitter-pattering feet on the floor and some rustling in the bedroom. It seems my husband and puppy dogs, Mr Anderson and Mr Oliver, are getting up. Mr Oliver comes walking out of the bedroom and then stops to stretch and yawn before he heads over for his routine bark with excitement to get me to go to the kitchen and cut him a piece of apple.

Oliver, the younger of our two 'puppies', as I like to call them, is an 11-year-old miniature pinscher that I swear is my soul twin. It fills me with great joy and laughter as I watch his little personality and am constantly reminded of myself. My little heart chakra on legs (credit goes to my friend, author and leading personal development personality, Arielle Ford for this perfect phrase).

After I've handed over the apple, Mr Anderson and my husband Timm come out from the bedroom and Mr Anderson stretches and yawns. However, for some reason, he likes to do it on my Yoga mat. The Downward Dog. He's the older of the two at 12 so his stretches seem to be a little longer and a little deeper and he, like my husband, is not as food-driven as Mr Oliver and I, so he just comes in for the snuggles.

Oh, how I love my mornings with my boys. They're so peaceful and often involve me reading to my husband over a few coffees before he heads off to his studio. But today was his day off and it was a beautiful sunny mild spring day. Perfect for a walk. Walks in my neighbourhood, though, had become a source of anxiety for me. But I went because I am aware how important it is for me and my puppies to move our bodies, especially because the majority of the time I am sitting behind my computer.

The reason I have lost interest in walking in my neighbourhood is because, like people, Mr Anderson and Mr Oliver are sensitive to our environment and other people. And because there are so many other dogs and people in my neighbourhood we have a few run-ins which are less than peaceful.

Maybe it's a little-dog thing, but they seem to turn into monster dogs when we meet other dogs and people. We even took them to dog school at which they were gold star dogs until we got home!

So walking them posed a consistent challenge for us and it was something that I did just to get it over with, making sure I took them to the same poles and spots where they liked to do their business as quick as I possibly could. I was never really present, enjoying the act or giving them the opportunity to either – always, almost literally sometimes, dragging them home as soon as I saw another dog coming our way.

But this day turns out to be a little different. I take Oliver and of course Timm takes Mr Anderson, our familiars. And as we are walking something peculiar happens, or at least peculiar to me.

My husband yells, 'Watch out, look at your feet!' And of course I automatically think 'snake', and that it's going to bite me or Oliver, and one of us is going to die. (There's that monkey mind again.) However, it wasn't a snake or anything that could harm us at all. In fact, they were tiny and fragile and for the entire nine years that I had lived here I had never seen them before, but I was about to be made aware that they had been there all along.

Tiny beautiful snails on the sidewalk were trying to cross over from one sanctuary of grass to another before the sun got too hot and dried them all up. But how strange. All these years I had never even noticed them. And there I stood watching my husband picking them up one by one and putting them on the other side of the grass. There were dozens and watching him help them all along was probably one of the most expanding things I have ever witnessed. Like the Grinch who stole Christmas, my heart grew two sizes that day.

And because I, and so many others that had been walking that path, had been so disconnected and concerned with 'getting something done' as opposed to really being present and enjoying the walk, not only did we do it with less presence but what we hadn't noticed was that we were walking on and killing dozens of tiny little creatures along the way.

This temporarily broke my heart and I felt a deep sense of guilt and shame that my lack of awareness cut short the lives of these innocent little creatures, who in themselves are a reminder to take things slow and steady with awareness.

When I returned home, I looked up the spiritual meaning of a snail to see if, besides the obvious lesson of awareness, there was another message this experience and these little creatures had for me. And lo and behold, they did.

The spiritual symbology of snails begins with the fact that they are spiritually known to bridge the gap of awareness between the physical and spiritual world (wisdom), and they carry their home, or one could say their innate spiritual wisdom, with them wherever they go. They also symbolize taking our time and enjoying the process.

***

AHA! There it is again. **Every time we stop, take it slow and live our life with presence, the truth of our awareness is right there for us to discover.** That is – if we pay attention. If not, just like me with the snails on the sidewalk, we go through life never knowing what kind of impact we've had on our environment and most importantly ourselves.

Living disconnected from ourselves, without presence, we never really quite enjoy life or even understand its purpose as we are far too busy trying to 'get it done' and miss out on the little creatures with big messages along the way.

A few days after, while I am enjoying my morning coffee outside on my balcony, I look down at my feet and there is a snail. Perhaps a little reminder from the universe of the lesson I had learned only days before, and to remember to live each day with that state of awareness. Not only on a walk with my dogs but in each and everything that I do, whether it's my morning shower, a conversation with a friend or even just watching a movie.

In this age of technology we seem to be distracted by everything, constantly with our faces in our phones. Perhaps, if we lift our heads for just a minute, we'll see that the life around us is constantly pointing to the wisdom within us.

The Practice of Awareness

Through the practice of awareness we cultivate the wisdom we need to draw closer to ourself, to feel ourself and our truth amongst the chaos of life. In every experience we make the conscious effort to know who we are and to facilitate our life from that awareness: to go left when we're guided left, to stand up when we're called to stand up and to walk out when we're called to walk out.

Cultivating that sense of awareness makes life's journey, and our purpose in it, a little clearer and enables us to focus on what really matters: the heart of the matter. With every choice that life presents us, we get clearer on the deepest intent embedded within our souls to be birthed.

Every experience in our lives seems to be calling us and we can choose either to listen or to ignore. If we listen we are gracefully set ablaze on a path that reflects our innermost desires, birthing a world that calls us higher. If we ignore and wait, perhaps we are shown over and over again through experiences that may not be so comfortable, each containing a whisper and then a scream calling us back to our own awareness. To our authentic selves.

Cultivating that intrinsic sense of awareness can be challenging. However, amongst the challenges there's that deep inner knowing that we came to life with, which along this journey we have allowed to become a distant memory. Perhaps being so enamoured with what seems like the right way or the right thing to do, and to realize later you were a victim of the human condition, selling your own soul so as not to be ostracized by the collective.

Whatever happened along the way, just like practicing Yoga makes you a better Yogi, then practicing awareness makes you more aware. But, as with everything in life, there are so many options. Like being at the market, surrounded by so many choices, perhaps each vendor has their own brand of lemon and by appearance they may all look similar, or taste similar – but which one to choose?

All these thoughts fill our heads when we are presented with choices. Conditioning takes over and we can at first be drawn to choose what's popular or be led by the vendor with the best sales pitch. In the end, though, we will only be truly satisfied if we give ourselves the space (solitude) to make the purchase or decision from our gut, intuition or inner awareness.

Do enjoy the fun of the market place, though, visiting all the vendors and then leaving with what calls to you most. And the same applies to our daily practices and the practice of awareness. Every guru, teacher, article and friend will have an idea as to what's best for us and perhaps we may need to try them all out in an attempt to discover our own. **There is no right or wrong way. There is only the way you choose, and eventually you'll be led to the right one for you.**

Self-Inquiry

Self-inquiry is the process of constantly checking in with ourselves – finding the meaning, or the purest intention, behind our actions and asking ourselves why. Why did I react (a conditioned response) rather than respond (a true behaviour from our deepest self)? Where is that coming from? And then being still long enough to hear the answer.

And when the answer arises, going deeper by asking more questions of ourselves. Often in life we don't know why we react or respond. We act from an unconscious place which creates both inner and outer conflicts as we are out of alignment with who we are, our truth. Perhaps reacting is what we were conditioned to do through witnessing others as we grew. Maybe we witnessed our parents in conflict, triggering each other and then hitting back (reacting) like a ping-pong match. Then without questioning we mirrored the same in our own relationships, never truly being still to identify the state of our own awareness and what we truly wanted, but reacting from a place of conditioned response to our triggered emotions. This example is a perfect place to begin self-inquiry, to give ourselves the space to step back and ask: 'What's happening here?', 'Why am I being triggered?' and 'What is it that I want them to understand?' And then respond from that state of awareness.

I know that for many years in my life I never truly took the time to self-inquire, to check in with myself and ask what I was really feeling and what I really wanted to communicate. Instead I reacted from my triggers, causing much chaos in my life and the lives of others and causing myself and others undue pain and suffering, even costing me some very important relationships.

Self-inquiry is a simple practice which doesn't really require much time. Mostly you'll get the answer sooner than you expect if you just give yourself the space to be still and listen, but in the case of a disagreement (as in the example above) it does require that we are clear in stating our boundaries and communicating that we need the space to get clear before we respond.

However, self-inquiry is not just a practice in our relationships to other people, but most importantly in our relationship in knowing ourselves. Self-inquiry is my religion. **Whenever I am struggling to find an answer, whether it's which way to go, what to choose or how to respond, I take a step back and give myself the space and time I need to dig deep – and question, question, question until the truth is revealed.**

Mindful Movement

Mindful movement immediately reminds me of Tai Chi, something that I have not yet personally experienced; however, I saw it in action on the lawn of the parliament buildings in Victoria, British Columbia while on my way to Beacon Hill Park to write the first words for this book. (I swear I saw Margaret Atwood there – the perfect omen for this book.)

We are constantly moving our bodies, but most of the time – like our minds – without awareness. We open our eyes and jump out of bed, most of the time without even being aware that we're shocking our system, never giving our bodies the chance to catch up with our minds. And, in turn, we are moving contrary to our natural rhythm.

Mindful movement is the practice of moving with awareness. Mentally focusing on every movement of our body and then facilitating that with the intention of our inner awareness. There are many slow, steady and focused Yoga practices that facilitate mindful movement – though Power Yoga is not one of them.

While Tai Chi is a form of mindful movement that is picking up speed as a practice to help anyone from seniors to corporate executives reconnect with themselves, we don't need a name or classroom to practice mindful movement. We can incorporate it in our everyday lives, in baby steps (pun intended!). I like to do it barefoot in the forest, focusing on my footsteps as I walk along the path – lifting my feet and putting them down ever so gently as to 'kiss the earth with my feet', as the Buddhist monk Thich Nhat Hanh calls it. As opposed to just stomping through the path unaware not only of the effect of my thunderous stance on my own physical, mental and spiritual wellbeing, but of the impact I am having on the earth and what's growing from it.

Mindful movement brings me back to the awareness that we're all connected and, if I am paying attention, I notice what I need to notice to walk with intention and to be mindful of myself and the impact I am having on the whole.

Meditation

Ah, that word again. As you know, it's not my favourite practice; however, maybe I just haven't found the method that works best for me yet, or maybe I have and I'm holding it against some idea that was presented to me versus realizing that Meditation is a means for understanding (myself) versus a perfect method.

There are so many methods of Meditation. Through Yoga teacher training I learned many; however, in the last few years since I 'graduated' I have read and experienced many more. There are too many to include here, but the purpose of them all is to be still and to gain a deeper understanding of ourselves and the meaning of our lives.

One type of Meditation I used to really enjoy is a Walking Meditation. In Yoga teacher training we would all get in a circle, close our eyes, put one hand on another's shoulder and then walk, being mindful of our every movement. Sometimes I would slip into somewhat of a trance and either effortlessly go with the flow or end up causing a catastrophe and setting everyone off course. In which case I always found myself in a fit of mischievous laughter, triggering old memories of being disruptive in class and ending up with my nose against the wall in the hallway. But it's all part of the process, right? So I take a deep breath, forgive myself and then back at it I go.

A type of Meditation that seemed to work better for me was Focused Meditation. In this practice I would use a candle, although I was always paranoid I would burn down the house, so I made sure there was no paper around or anything that could spontaneously catch fire. Once I made sure all was safe I would place the candle on the floor about two feet in front of me, sit comfortably cross-legged and turn my attention or focus to the candle. After a few minutes the candle would 'disappear' and my vision was encompassed with pure light. The light always gave me a sense of warmth and peace, and when I finished the Meditation a spontaneous sense of awareness and creativity seemed to come out of nowhere. However, I am now aware that this nowhere is somewhere within my own soul. The place that 'passeth understanding' but holds the key to my intrinsic sense of awareness, the deepest intent or meaning behind everything I am.

And last but not least, one of my favourite guided meditations – that reminds me of being a little boy winding down for bed being read a story by caring elders – is Oprah Winfrey and Deepak Chopra's 21-Day Meditation Experience. Although I struggle with the commitment to do it every day, when I do get an opportunity to listen to them I always come out with a profound inner wisdom and a desire to apply that wisdom in every aspect of my life. My favourite of the many of their free offerings was the 'Hope in Uncertain Times' piece. It really helped me to gain the perspective to sit behind my thoughts, to feel that place Gary Zukav calls 'The Seat of the Soul' and to understand that all is well in my world. It allowed me the space to know that I didn't have to be unsettled by the inner worldly drama projecting outward, and that I could use that state of deep inner peace to create more in my life, and then to inspire others on the path as well.

The key is in the practice, and the consistency. Maybe we don't choose the same practice every day but we practice every day because we owe to ourselves and the world the gift of our own higher awareness, and instead of projecting our pain we are unconsciously bringing awareness to it and through it and realizing we're all in this together.

Reflection: Are You Ready to Reveal the Light?

Awareness is something that seems to be constantly tugging at our heart strings, leading the way for a life in alignment with our deepest truth. Every experience is an opportunity for us to know that place on a deeper level and to give from that space, with every action creating a sort of 'domino effect' within our environment and hopefully through the world.

Whatever experience it takes us to find that place, it is unique to us. Some people seem to get it very early in life and for some it takes the involvement in a tragic accident or near death. No one way is right or wrong, each being a unique set of events that chip away at what's clouded our hearts, eventually exposing the light of inner awareness that was there all along.

As there are experiences that reveal the light, there are also experiences which muddle it. And such is the journey – each of us with a path of our own, with a story of our own, with experiences that make or break us.

But amongst it all we have the choice. We can let life's experiences harden us, we can build walls of protection or suits of armour, or we can let them break us open and leave us vulnerable to reveal to ourselves and those around us the deepest secrets that lie within.

Right there, in that place, in that vulnerable place of the awareness of our own inner light, we begin to experience what freedom feels like and perhaps light the way for others to experience the same. When we share our own awareness, we take a more powerful step in our own healing and bring greater connection and community into our lives.

CHAPTER 3

YOUR WORTHINESS IS NOT AN OUTSIDE THING – WORTH

I sit here on my balcony contemplating the question: what is worthiness? I hold a cigarette in one hand, I'm wearing a baseball cap, and my mind is running amok with memories of the past and thoughts of what my future looks like.

Recently my life has taken a direction that is less than desirable, but desirable to who? If I was to choose a religion, mine would be self-inquiry. I am constantly questioning – where did that thought come from? What's influencing my actions?

And then I look at the cigarette burning away and I look up at people walking by. Thoughts fill my head again. But now they seem to be attached to how smoking this cigarette somehow has something to do with my worth. How wearing this cap to cover up my thinning hair is a reflection of my worth. And how the thoughts I'm having about my future and what that will look like are asking me: am I, or will I be, worthy?

Are these my thoughts, or are they 40 years of other people's thoughts interfering with my own inner voice? And at the core of that voice, my own self-worth. And here comes the anxiety that has so aggressively sat down at life's table unwelcome for my entire life, the conditioned thoughts that I can't help but hear. And then I pivot back and forth between throwing it out on its ass and screaming 'fuck you', to inviting it in for a cup of tea, and allowing it to be listened to.

Asking these thoughts, 'Which is really me?', 'What's coming up for me?', 'What's my story?' And then listening with the awareness that I have worked on for my entire adult life.

Be still and know, Shayne, be still and know …

I know because I'm sitting here about to delve into the topic of worthiness that it must absolutely be the subject, and because I've struggled with it my entire life, and I – we all – really so desperately want to be free from it, to be valued and for the world (and ourself) to accept us just the way we are.

But it's not been the case. We learn this at an early age, sometimes as early as our first memories trying to pick out our own clothes that didn't match, or weren't gender specific enough, and the voice of our parent or guardian speaking up, gently or sometimes not so gently, 'people will laugh at you', 'boys/girls don't wear that'. And then you feel a sinking in your soul.

We don't want to be looked at as not belonging, and we so desperately want our parents and peers to see and love us. And there it begins. We bargain for love (our worthiness) by showing up the way we're 'supposed to', and suppressing our innermost selves in the process.

We've not applied for but accepted the position of worthless – it is not something that is forced upon us, but we accept it. It's created in our head when we fail to tick off the labels of society, when we fail to receive the gold star of approval. You know the gold star, right? The one you perhaps received on your first assignment as a child? Or perhaps you didn't and then there was that sinking feeling again, and the birth of your desire to get that gold star at whatever cost, even at the cost of not being yourself.

It's all too familiar for me and its grip tightened as I began to grow. Because deep inside I knew I was so radically different than 'the norm'. However, I knew that in order to survive, at least in that world, I would have to conform. I would have to wait in the line with everyone else, in the hope of receiving my gold star. And if I didn't I would then have to pay enough attention to figure out what it was I had to do to get it.

Even today I catch myself looking to my peers, within my genre, to see what's acceptable, what's trending, to see what it takes to receive my gold star. Or in today's language, social media likes and shares.

And it's painful, oh so painful. And it changes so rapidly that it's a whirlwind of anxiety just trying to keep up. And a distraction from the reality that is who I really am now, and a deep inner knowing that my worthiness is not an outside thing.

And somehow I've known this all along. It's a voice that's travelled with me from aged five (my earliest memory) until today – nearly 40 years later. Sometimes it's been a whisper and most recently it's been shouts, shouts so loud it's impossible not to listen.

'Who am I? Who are you?'

Who are we without the conditioning that we've allowed to dictate our worthiness? And what even is this word we call worth?

The dictionary describes worth as 'the value equivalent to that of someone or something under consideration; the level at which someone or something deserves to be valued or rated'. But under consideration by who? Deserving to be valued or rated by who? Who is this person or group of persons who decides our worth or what or who is valued?

But as children the dictionary seems to have become our dictator of authority. Or perhaps if we grew up in a religious household, that religion or whatever theology our family adopted became that authority as well. Above our own inherent voice or truth, we started our lives handing over authority to words above feelings (our inner voice), to other people's truths rather than our own. But we trusted them because, hey, they knew, right?

Or did they, do they? Does anybody really know? Or can anybody really know who we truly are, or what is right for us?

We're born into family units, and blindly trust that they have our best interests at heart. We then board the bus to institutions such as schools, churches and libraries governed by collective theologies and rules by which to live, perhaps never even questioning if they are right for us.

Or when we do, we end up with our nose against the wall, or in my case sat under a desk facing an entire class in shame. And when we don't question, when we follow the rules, when we dress how we're supposed to dress, act how we're supposed to act and hand in our papers in the perfect form, we get the gold star.

Or as adults that gold star becomes accolades, admiration, career advancement, things and money. For some reason a puppet comes to mind and the strings bear the names of every theology and rule that's controlling our lives which we so desperately want to cut.

But what if we fall? What if we can't stand by ourselves?

And that scares the shit out of us. Because up until this point we've been safe. We've been supported by the 'norms' because we've allowed them to carry us, and to break free from that may mean that we no longer have support, that we are no longer worthy, and that's what we've been afraid of our entire lives. Not being seen, not being part of the collective, being thrown out in the storm with no protection. Or if we take a tour through history, tied up and burned at the stake, literally burning our worth and taking our lives with it.

Perhaps today it's not legal to burn us at the stake, but it doesn't mean it's not happening. Maybe it's not so literal. The sticks have turned to words, and the fires turned to an inferno of loneliness, where our worthiness dies to the world as we know it and we're forced into mental purgatory. And for those who are not so resilient, that could still mean death (suicide).

I contemplated that path once; well, many times, once even almost succeeding. However, once I awoke, wiped my lips of charcoal, looked around and saw no one there, just me alone, I had an awakening … a rush of life, and an awareness that I am it. I am whatever words follow, I am. That life begins and ends with me, that I went to sleep alone, and I woke up alone, and that everything, everyone and every experience was a mirror reflecting back to me the opportunity to stand up like a lion and roar and when I did the world began to listen.

That day I cut the strings that almost killed me, stood on my own two feet, and began the journey to the awareness that my worthiness was not an outside thing. **However, like any realization, beginning with learning to walk, we first scoot on our bums, then crawl, stand up, wobble and then run.**

Some of us walk at six months, some at nine, and, well, me, I was more interested in food and so too chubby to stand, so I crawled and crawled until I gained the inner strength to realize that however heavy life is, I could stand, I could walk and I could run.

Because whatever force was responsible for that wasn't outside, but within. And such is our worthiness.

Sometimes life can feel like a game of 'pin the tail on the donkey'. We've been blindfolded, spun around and then pushed to find ourselves. There are people shouting, 'this way', 'no, this way', but the only way we will find our way is to be still enough to remember, and with that awareness, drown out the noise and take baby steps towards it.

Take a walk back through your life to an experience when you were five years old. Or 10 or 12. Or perhaps 16 when you got your first job, and then you lost it. Perhaps you were 17 and you went on your first date, and they didn't show up. Or 18 and you got your final college paper stamped with a D, or 21 and you just found the confidence to tell your circle of friends who you really are, or 29 and you're losing your hair, 40 and you find your first wrinkle, 50 and you start to go grey, 60 and so on.

Where within those experiences did you give away your worth? When did you start believing you were not good enough, not educated enough, and didn't know how … Where did you hand your value over to others, or your idea of how you're supposed to be or what your life was supposed to look like? Where did you consciously or unconsciously surrender and hand your worth over to the collective? **If we don't define our own worth, others define it for us.**

It's time we shifted our focus from outside to inside, and when we're not feeling worthy ask ourselves what it is, or better yet who it is, whose thoughts and ideas we are believing? And then centre back to believing ourself.

There are so many excuses that create the resistance to knowing our own worth. Like poison we've collected along the path to our own awareness, but what we need to be reminded is that we are the force within that makes the decision to drink it. And that without its intoxication we know that we've always been worthy, we were born worthy.

This now is our opportunity to embrace the extreme power of the self that is gained with self-inquiry, to look to cleanse our outside around us and to release our own beliefs about ourselves and our worth.

My Story: He Spoke to Me in My Dreams

'Within each of us is another whom we do not know, and (s)he speaks to us in our dreams.'

Carl Jung

This quote nails it. He spoke to me in my dreams. My whole life from the time I can remember I dreamed of writing, I would write poetry from my heart but was graded poorly, I would write plays and ideas for television that were reality versus soap operas (which were popular at the time) to feedback that my reality was too heavy, to dreams of travelling the world learning about other cultures and making what difference I could, to thoughts that I was a poor boy from the ghetto who wasn't worthy. However, beyond the conditioning of my unworthiness and the resistance that bullied me, sometimes into submission, was innate curiosity, a powerful desire to achieve it all, and the gift of resilience.

And one day I woke up from that dream to realize I could make it a reality, but what awoke with that dream was a monster that I call unworthiness.

I was wearing a suit that I had purchased at a swanky downtown store, looking out of my office window and realized 'this is not my life'. I had the car, the money, the loft, but somehow I felt an emptiness inside of me. A depression set in, a not-so-distant stranger. I've experienced this before, except last time it looked like a prison, was full of students and almost led to my death. But this time it wasn't being inflicted on me by others. It was my own choices that led me here.

My choices were choices that were led by a desire to prove my worth. I chose to acquire everything that was perceived as success so that I could walk into my high school reunion (something like Romy and Michele) and say, 'Look, I am worthy,' 'I'm the king of the world,' 'I've got the job, the money and everything that I need to look and feel powerful and you can't take my worth from me anymore.'

My worth was from the outside (things), and in the process I had completely been disconnected from what was inside. Because success (worth) defined by the collective looked like money and things but what was knocking at my window as I looked out of my office that day was the truth.

My dreams, my true desires, my destiny was calling to me that day and because I was too afraid to listen, for fear of stepping outside of what I believed held my worth, I didn't listen. I kept it up. I kept getting in the car, that led to the job, that brought me the money, that dictated my worth. And every day that knock would get louder and louder and my depression deeper and deeper.

I would spend evenings trying to suppress the voice with drugs and alcohol and long drives into the city wiping my tears. Until one day, the pain of remaining in a life that wasn't my truth was more than the fear of being perceived as unworthy. And on that very day I sat in my office with my head down, and anxiety so bad I felt like I was going to pass out.

Thoughts were running through my head, 'What would I do?', 'I won't have any money', 'What will people think?' and then I would go deeper, inquire to the depths of my soul. 'Whose voice was this?' And I remembered the book I had been reading that was the catalyst to a deeper self-awareness: *The Four Agreements* by Don Miguel Ruiz: 'Be impeccable with your word,' 'Use the power of your word in the direction of truth'; 'Don't take anything personally,' 'What others say and do is a projection of their own reality'; 'Don't make assumptions,' 'Communicate with others as clearly as you can to avoid misunderstandings,' and 'Always do your best.' 'Under any circumstance, simply do your best.'

I closed my laptop, packed up my bag, went home and wrote my resignation letter. I spoke my truth with conviction, without the fear of how it would be received, and with no mind chatter about what would happen, how they would see me, or how I would be seen by others. In that moment I felt so alive, so deeply in connection with myself and with a sense of ease that from that day forth doing my best was good enough, and if that meant jumping from a corporate career that I felt defined my worth, and falling through mental purgatory until I found solid ground again, so be it. Because at that time what was most important to me was being impeccable with my word, and standing in the power of my own truth. Whatever that looked like. But what I knew for sure was that it wasn't in that office.

Days passed by as my employer questioned my decision, and even questioned my sanity. But I was determined to follow my truth and embark upon the journey to defining my worth from the inside out.

Not without a lot of struggle. There were so many moments when deep panic took hold of me, leaving me feeling suffocated at times, not able to catch the breath I needed to survive. Day by day the reality set in as my bank account began to drain, as I watched the bills pile in from the life they used to sustain.

The pressure to cave in and go back became so strong, to surrender to the collective idea or worth versus having the courage to uncover my own. I watched everything fade away – the money, the car … and then finally the trip to the bank to bankrupt the life I'd left behind and embark upon a deeply spiritual path to discovering my own self-worth.

***

It was a journey not for the faint of heart and, had resilience not been my superpower, I'm not sure I'd be writing this today. However, whenever I have listened to the whispers (or screams … I was a little stubborn) they have always led me in the direction of my highest good.

Sometimes – ok, a lot of the time – I was kicking and screaming, and resisting … choosing 'vthe school of hard knocks. But looking back from the awareness I have now, and the fullness of my self-worth, which I'm still working on, I wouldn't change a thing.

Even though my worth is challenged daily, I've gained the awareness to put my monkey mind into perspective, put down the poison and drink from my own cup of worth.

The Practice of Self-Worth

Self-Inquiry
Self-inquiry is the practice of constantly bringing our attention to our own inner awareness. This practice was introduced to me by American-born spiritual teacher Gangaji and has since been my religion. In any situation, be it a conflict or new direction, I give myself the space to practice asking myself questions and being still enough to hear the answers.

At first this practice can be a mind struggle. Every thought and idea about ourselves that we've been conditioned to think runs amok in our heads and can sometimes be very convincing that it's our truth.

But if you keep sitting, keep asking, and keep being still and listening, as the loud voices of others (conditioning) begin to fade you will slowly and clearly begin to hear your own voice and then act from there.

I often refer to this as conscious action versus reaction. Reaction most often comes from a place of conditioning, using our past experiences to dictate our current reality, and is often a heightened, sometimes aggressive and angry energy not connected to our truth or in alignment with our self-worth or value.

Responding with conscious action is always in alignment with our highest value or self-worth. We've stopped and listened long enough to tap into our inner awareness, to sift through our triggers, past stories and grievances to connect to the truth of our highest good, and from our highest place of self-worth our reactions or responses convey our self-worth.

Looking Your Best

Looking my best always makes me feel my best. And this doesn't mean conforming to what others' versions of your best are. It's about you, standing in front of your own mirror, comfortable in your own skin.

It's amazing how incredible we feel about ourselves just by simply grooming – getting a haircut, a manicure, or showering daily. Especially showering daily! I know when I've gotten into ruts of depression I've gone a few days without showering, and more than a month without a haircut and it definitely affected how I felt about myself. The moment I stepped out of the salon I felt like I could take on the world again. And that was just from grooming.

It's also so very important to be comfortable in what we are wearing. Because the more comfortable we are the more confident we are. I have tried so many trending styles; however, when I looked in the mirror I felt as if I was wearing a costume. It didn't look or feel like me, and anytime I went against those feelings and left the house things didn't work out for me. Whether it was the level of my engagement at a social event or a meeting, people can tell when you lack self-worth and confidence. It's almost as if you're wearing it on your t-shirt.

Part of feeling comfortable in your clothes and in your body is keeping healthy, whatever that looks and feels like for you. When I am looking and feeling my healthiest I am so alive and it seems that things just work out better for me.

And I'm prepared to look my best, to feel my best to get the best. However, I get the struggle. But looking your best wherever you're at is kind of like gratitude. The more you do it the more you have to be grateful for. So whatever shape you're in, start by perfecting that and work in baby steps from there.

And always wear a smile. It's contagious.

Trusting Yourself and Your Desires

This kind of goes hand-in-hand with self-inquiry. It's the answers that come when we sit and listen. And then the courage to trust what comes up. I know. It can be challenging to sort out what's yours and what's not, especially when you've been running on conditioned auto-pilot for your entire life.

It can be scary because when what's coming up for you is incongruent with your current reality it may require an entire life shift. So many people in my life over the past few years have come to this realization, and when they do, the resistance kicks up hard. It begins a sometimes overwhelming rush of self-evaluation.

Who am I really?

Am I this house, this car, this job, this marriage?

And if we've never stopped long enough to ask such simple questions, the shit can get real and quick, often hitting all our triggers at once, forcing us to pay attention and then act accordingly.

But it's challenging when our whole lives have been dictated by the lust of gaining our self-worth from conditioned values and desires versus our own, and it seems from my experience that upon this type of awakening old systems and relations fall apart to make way for what's real.

And during that process we may have the involuntary reaction to dig our nails into the pavement and try to hold onto our past for dear life, for fear of the unknown. However, from my own personal experience and that of my dear friends, you need to 'let go or be dragged' (a Zen proverb). **If you don't have the courage to listen to your own voice and desires, you will end up in a life that, like an outfit, never quite feels like it fits.** And the longer you sit in that uncomfortable space the more uncomfortable it gets.

So the best thing you can do for yourself is to listen to yourself, and take baby steps towards the whispers of your deepest desires. I say baby steps solely because first, that's what works for me, and second, remember that you didn't get into a disconnected life overnight, so you won't get out of it that way either.

Self-Appreciation

When I think about Self Appreciation I giggle, both because of the conditioning I have floating around in my head that we're not supposed to be proud, and it reminds me of an interview I did for my MyVividLife web series with author and financial wellness expert Kate Northrup (you can watch it at VividLife.me) where I spoke about affirmations.

'I love myself, I love myself, I love myself; no, I don't, I hate myself.'

Not quite funny that I hate myself, and at the core I really don't; however, what I was trying to relay is that unless you actually believe it to be true it's not going to penetrate your resistance to your own self-worth.

We have to believe and feel this with all our hearts, which is why with a self-appreciation practice I would suggest starting out small. Perhaps begin each day not looking in the mirror, although that little girl on YouTube makes it look epic (search for Jessica's 'Daily Affirmation' on YouTube). I think starting with a pen and paper, or a fancy leather-bound Harry Potter-looking journal in my case, and writing down one thing every day for a week that you appreciate about yourself is a good place to start. **As I'm writing I keep hearing the line from the movie _The Help_ in my head: 'You is smart. You is kind. You is important.'** It just makes me smile and a smile is a good place to start.

Choose something that makes you feel light in the heart, and remember it doesn't always have to be physical. We seem to always jump to our physical appearance when thinking of our self-worth, when we know that our worthiness is not an outside thing, it's an inside one.

So perhaps start with what personality trait you most love about yourself. Mine is that I love my ability to see the good in others no matter how they present. You could also be more in-depth and write an 'appreciate paragraph' that highlights your favourite personality trait and then gives examples through your story.

I love to write, so that would be my choice. And the more in-depth we are, the more details, the more we activate that inner voice that knows and then sometimes invokes a river of self-appreciation we never even knew was there.

So go ahead, give it a try. What do you most appreciate about yourself?

Good Vibe Tribe

We are a reflection of the people we spend our lives with. Think about that for a moment. Look around. Who's sitting at your table and what do they reflect to you?

I've done this many times in my life. In my younger days the process could be pretty volatile, involved a lot of projection and alienated a lot of people. I wasn't yet seasoned emotionally, didn't even have a clue. I just knew something wasn't right and those surrounding me didn't make me feel how I wanted to feel. It was never that I felt better than them, it was always that I felt bigger than the sum of the actions by the majority, and so I would move on.

As I grew and began to value myself more, so did the people in my tribe. They say your vibe attracts your tribe, or as others might say, you attract the people you have in your life based on how you're projecting or reflecting your life. And the clearer we get, the higher our sense of worth and the less we will attract people into our lives that don't align with that.

However, like negative thoughts, negative people can slip into our lives and it's our responsibility to 'pay attention to the whispers' and act accordingly. It may seem that it never lets up. No matter how much we're in alignment and value ourselves, negative people and experiences creep into our life.

I believe perhaps they're reminders to listen, to value that voice, to speak it and to act on it. But I also believe that these people could come into our experience to learn from us and so I'm not always so quick to 'throw the baby out with the bathwater'.

Not everyone needs to show up polished to perfection as we are all perfectly imperfect, but what is most important is that the people that we invite to our table mirror our highest worth (or vibes) and that if we're constantly neglectful of that, we must learn to get up from the table.

Reflection: Is this Right for Me?

Self-worth. Self-worth. Self- worth. That is the question. Where do we find it, and how are we defined by it?

It's an inside job. A place that due to the conditioning of our lives can be difficult to access, but with practice unlocks a magical force within us that aligns us with our highest good. We look to our stories, our ancestors, our teachers, our culture and even our neighbours to define it.

But, like Dorothy in *The Wizard of Oz*, we go on an outward journey only to discover it within. **And such is life, as I often say: 'every experience is walking us home**

to ourselves', and I believe we need those experiences to mirror to us where to look.

It was all so innocent – the process of following the leader because we trusted they knew the way, and perhaps they thought they did, and perhaps they did know but they could only know what was true for themselves. We start out students in life and we are so quick to graduate to teachers, most often without even mastering the subject ourselves. I refer to myself as a student of life and always will; sure there are some following me as how I've turned my tragedies to triumph inspires them, but like them I am still learning, still growing and through experiences always shifting my perception.

I keep an open heart and open mind. Never limiting myself to the thoughts and opinions laid before me and always taking life's big and little questions to self-inquiry. This, to me, is the ultimate amplification of self-worth – to value ourselves enough to check in with ourselves constantly. Is this right for me?

It's no different than our relationships with others, if we're in it together we consult with them before we make decisions. Is this right for you? And then if not, we take it to deeper inquiry and if we're not in alignment we don't go that way.

So why not value ourselves the same? After all, life begins and ends with us. We go to bed and wake up with ourselves and if we're not valuing our own self over the collective, we're mirroring a disconnected world. Disconnection from self is disconnection from the whole. Spiritually I tend to believe that there is no place where one begins and the others ends, that we are all an extension of the creative force that exists within – and when surrendered to that truth we become an expression of it and by the law of attraction we give others permission to do the same.

So, give yourself permission to value yourself first and watch how that unfolds within your life and attracts to you the people, places and experiences you deserve and desire and to a life full with self-worth and the peace that passeth understanding.

CHAPTER 4

LETTING GO OF WHAT DOESN'T SERVE YOU – YOUR ENVIRONMENT

Letting go of the things that don't serve us is probably one of the biggest frontiers we have to face in uncovering our conditioning and walking in the direction of our authentic self. Our entire lives have been spent attracting people and things unconsciously, often never really checking in to see if they, or it, serve our highest good.

Perhaps we've taken the beaten path when it comes to deciding where we live, who our friends are and even how our personal space is designed. Did I choose that house or was it a decision that was made based on how it will make me look? Did I choose that couch or was it chosen for me? Who are these 'friends' that I'm surrounded with?

It's really about stopping and getting still enough to inquire within. Is this really what I want? Is this really serving me? And that goes for both people and things. It seems we become what and who we surround ourselves with.

Every time I think about letting go of what doesn't resonate with me, or if I'm having the conversation with friends or family, I am reminded of and refer to a scene from the movie *Labyrinth* with David Bowie – the junk yard scene. (If you haven't seen it you can YouTube it.) The main character, Sarah, meets a woman in a junk yard and she is covered in junk.

It is piled so high on her back that she is hunched over and very ragged-looking. As Sarah enters the junk lady's lair it begins to look like her own bedroom filled with her memories and childhood treasures. The junk lady begins to pile these treasures from the past onto Sarah's back in a similar fashion to her own. As Sarah realizes that it's all junk that is weighing her down and distracting her from her real mission or destiny, she is able to free herself and return to her path.

For me, as a child watching this, I didn't really understand the message fully. But as I grew within, and as I paid more attention to my life and the messages within it, I was reminded when I watched the film to let go of what was weighing me down, or not serving my highest good. And this can be a very difficult task, especially when we attach our things and relationships to experiences, memories or people in the past. Whether those experiences or memories bring us joy or sadness we hold onto them, perhaps because we're not yet ready to let go of what we attach to them.

However, in my experience the more we hold onto 'stuff', the less mental clarity we have and the more anxiety and suffering we experience in our lives. These relationships and things hold some sort of comfort for us, even when they are quite toxic and overruling our lives. We would rather endure the suffering than look for the freedom. Perhaps because that pattern we are in provides a sense of comfort and security? The familiar is far more comforting than what we see as the risks of an uncertain future.

And I totally get that. I think we all have this inclination to a certain degree. Even as I write this I am in the process of letting go of a life that's fitting a little too snugly and exploring a path that is more in alignment with the real me. However, this life that I am walking away from has served me well.

And what's next is the unknown – which our mind likes to create an abyss of drama around, which can spiral into bad decisions around holding on versus letting go.

So many thoughts, feelings and emotions come rushing in as we begin to let go of what's not serving us and walking in the direction of what does. Even the little things like perhaps just cleaning out our closets can be a daunting task, not just physically but emotionally as well. Just one shirt can bring memories rushing in. Perhaps memories we're not willing to let go of, or perhaps ones that send us into a spiral of negative self-talk and emotions.

Maybe you wore that shirt on your first date with your partner, and the reason for your closet reorganization is that you've recently separated. Or you've found an old belt that belonged to your father who recently passed away. Or perhaps you found a jacket that you wore to the hospital for your first baby or a pair of shoes you walked the Camino in.

Each thing or relationship attached to memories which invoke strong thoughts and emotions, whether positive or negative, we want to hold onto – perhaps as a porthole to the past or an attachment to a relationship. But we get to decide whether it stays or goes.

We evaluate this by feeling. By getting still and checking in with ourselves and really giving us the time and space to process the memories and emotions fully. Sometimes it's through tears or anger, and a lot of times it's through joy. But I allow all of the feelings their space, and when I come to the space once they've cleared, I make my decision from that place. I ask myself a simple question, from clarity, from that vivid space, and not distracted by temporary thoughts, stories and emotions but from the present. I ask myself, 'What will this bring to my future? Does it make my life heavier or lighter?'

Life can be so heavy without holding onto everything that's attached to an experience or memory and it's quite amazing the shifts we experience when we do let go. It feels like a huge weight has been taken off our shoulders and a new energy knocks on our door.

However, the reason for holding on is not always experience- or memory-based. It can often be that the relationships and the things in our life are holding and reflecting our 'value', our sense of self. And that we've given that away to something outside of ourselves. Maybe it's a car that makes you feel important or a house in a prestigious neighbourhood, or even a spouse or friend that you've given your value over to. Whatever it is, you've placed your value in outside things versus yourself and so to let go of what doesn't serve you includes those relationships and possessions as well. And just because you've always found value in material things, or allowed your relationships to dictate your value, doesn't mean you need to sell the car or obliterate your relationship. Perhaps it's just an awareness and a shift in perception.

My dear friend, the author and meditation expert Ed Shapiro, once said to me, 'If you have things, you're good … if things have you, there's work to do there.' And that has always stayed with me through many of the major decisions I've made since.

Do I have it or does it have me?

Do you have it or does it have you?

Ask yourself? Are you calling the shots here? Are you in control or is it/are they in control of you?

And we always want to be in control. Not in control of others or things, but in control of ourselves. To have the wisdom to be able to discern in any given moment to let go of what doesn't serve us. And in letting go of what no longer serves us, we welcome what does.

My Story: A Box of Memories

There's an old ten-pound margarine container sitting in my in-laws' storage room, and in that box are years and years of things I've collected that have memories and meaning for me. There's a little yarn star that was made for me by one of my first roommates, there's love letters from my first crush, pictures from my sixteenth birthday party, flyers from a series of shows I used to produce at the local bar, old programs from high school plays I was in, and a picture from the first play I wrote and directed as a preteen. All bring back memories and invoke a rollercoaster of emotions that both trigger and inspire me.

I've been moving this container from house to house since I was about 16, as well as carrying them in my heart. Each time I open it I bring those experiences to life. Some of them so painful they send me into a downward spiral that has often left me bedridden, lacking the motivation to even move – sometimes for just a day, and sometimes it lasts days on end where it's an effort for me to just get up and shower.

A ten-pound margarine box of memories I've carried around from place to place for almost 30 years has in theory, and when revisited, caused an immense amount of suffering. Every time I open that box I am taken into each memory one by one but in a new way with a different perspective. My old perspective or conditioning has a way of creeping in and whispering self-defeating thoughts in my head.

'You weren't good enough to get the main role,' 'If only you'd had the courage to sing,' 'If only you'd kept doing events,' 'But if you hadn't said that to her,' 'If you'd just changed one thing you could bring them back,' 'Look what you could have been had you not ...'

You know the thoughts. I'm sure you have them every time you take a trip down memory lane. And not every experience was negative, but as you look back they can twist into unrecognizable stories. Our thoughts, as Alan Watts said, are 'a good servant, but a bad master'. They run amok, melting stories of our past with our current reality and perception, feeding our self-limiting minds and beating us up over and over again with the thoughts of 'what could have been ...'

I'm not sure what possible power constantly looking at our past could have on our present and our future. I've visited this place, through this container many, many times and been thrown back into trauma each time. Iyanla Vanzant, host of *Iyanla Fix My Life* on OWN TV, says ...

until you heal the wounds of your past, you will continue to bleed. You can bandage the bleeding with food, with alcohol, with drugs, with work, with cigarettes, with sex, but eventually, it will all ooze through and stain your life. You must find the strength to open the wounds, stick your hands inside, pull out the core of the pain that is holding you in your past, the memories, and make peace with them.

And conditioning would have us put the memories one-by-one back into the box and under the stairs, only to keep revisiting them over and over through emotions which never let go of us until we allow them the space to move and to heal. I used to bandage them with cigarettes, work, drugs, alcohol – and the biggest one, the one I use even to this day to bandage what I don't want or am too tired to heal – food. I open the box of memories, up come the emotions, down goes the bag of chips and dip.

But then an AHA moment hit me right in the root chakra (life foundation/support) when I read these words from author and emotional eating expert Geneen Roth:

'We eat the way we eat because we are afraid to feel what we feel.'

And from that moment forth every time I went to binge eat a bag of chips and dip or eat an entire box of cookies, I remembered her words. Sometimes I would keep eating but most of the time I would give myself permission to dig deeper, 'to stick my hand inside and pull out the core of the pain'. Man, was it difficult. My conditioning shouting: 'boys don't cry', and 'you'll relapse and end up back in the hospital'. But courage would overtake the voices and rock my cradle, rock it back and forth until I was calm enough to put it all into perspective and rip and burn that memory literally and metaphorically.

Later on my path, burning symbols of my distress would become an important ritual for me in clearing the past to make way for a more peaceful present and a vivid vision of the path before me. Although not before I allowed myself to process and make peace with the emotions, because I found when I burned a memory before I had fully processed it, it would keep coming back to haunt me over and over again until I did.

Not everyone has the capacity to revisit memories through attachments; whether physical, relational or metaphorical. Meditation and self-inquiry are my way, and resilience and vulnerability seem to be my superpowers. However, if you don't feel you can do this alone safely, I suggest you work with a psychotherapist.

When I finally had the realization that my past, attached to experiences through relationships or things, was keeping me from a peaceful and healthy present I reached out to a psychotherapist as I knew at this point it was too overwhelming and I didn't have the strength to go it alone.

After very few sessions I was able to gain the courage to share my story, the wounds that kept me prisoner to them and the margarine box of memories, and one by one, with practice and patience, watch them burn baby burn. I was able to let go of what no longer served me, holding the wisdom I gained from each experience, feeling the peace that comes with clarity and holding a clearer vision of who I was without the pain, and a brighter lighter future ahead.

***

To this day I practice letting go of what doesn't serve me in every area of my life, from food and clothes to people; and it's such a mystical magical experience because every time I do, something, or someone, shows up to light the way for a new awareness.

And now I prepare to move house again. Ten years of memories from our annual holiday soirées where we fit 50 people in 650 square feet, to tea parties, sleepovers, family days in the pool, Mother's Day brunches, walks on the beach, sunrises over the marina and sunsets on our balcony with friends.

So many laughs, epic memories and also tears. I lost three of the most important people in my life while living in this home, beginning just a week before we moved in: my cousin and one of my best friends, Kim. Then one year later almost to the day, my Grandmother Dorothy (like *The Wizard of Oz*), and just a few months ago my brother (and only sibling), Chris.

A home is not just bricks and mortar, or these days chipwood and siding, but a vessel that houses our most intimate moments and cherished memories with those closest to our hearts. And although I'm going to miss this place, my gypsy soul's screaming that it's time to move this wagon on. And as the pictures flash through my mind I'm reminded how blessed I have been to have experienced this all, and I can hardly wait for what's next.

The Practice of Letting Go

Letting go takes practice and, as the old saying goes, 'practice makes perfect', right? Well, sort of – if you believe in perfect the way we were conditioned to believe. But perfect to me is where I am at. Wherever that is. That's if I'm in alignment with my who, what, when, why, where and how … and even when I'm not, perhaps that experience is an opportunity to align.

But I do know that there are certain practices that have helped me and my good vibe tribe let go. Whether it was clothes that were cluttering up their closest or a relationship that didn't serve our highest good. These practices are great tools.

Awareness

Awareness to me comes through self-inquiry and talking. It's very practical. Too many theologies tend to confuse me so I like to just check in with my own inner guru. But first I like to meditate to clear the slate. My go-to meditation is my barefoot walking in the woods.

I start by taking off my shoes and socks, and then closing my eyes and feeling the earth on my bare feet, I then put one foot in front of the other, conscious of my heel hitting the earth, and then the front of my foot. I think, as Thich Nhat Hanh says, that I'm 'kissing the earth' with my feet, mindful of the impact I'm having on the earth and feeling as if we are one. More hocus pocus, I know … but it's not so hocus pocus. Do a little research on the mind-body benefits of barefooting and I guarantee you'll be getting kicked out of grocery stores in your near future.

This exercise is both a meditation and a practice of awareness. It slows down the mind and limits the mind drama, and allows us the space to get clear. From this space we can gain the awareness of what our attachments are, and why we have them.

While in Yoga teacher training I learned a valuable meditation for letting go of attachments that were causing me suffering. It was simple yet profound.

This instructor said a few simple words that felt like they took years of tension and pressure off my chest in an instant: 'Allow it to be and it will pass.'

No more conflict with my thoughts, attachments and emotions: I could just let them be, let them have their space in my awareness and they would pass on their own.

I know it sounds like hocus pocus, new age bull, right? But what are hocus pocus and new age anyway, but theologies meant to ease our suffering? Whatever path works for us works, and we get to choose that path. **Whether we choose oracle cards or a walk in the woods, all paths lead home.**

Loving What Is

'Loving what is'. Self-acceptance or acceptance. This is all the same idea: the practice of loving ourselves wherever we're at, like the meditation I learned in Yoga teacher training, 'Allow it to be and it will pass.' Again, it's not a fix-all or a bypass, but just one of the many tools we can utilize to assist us in life and in letting go.

We're not all operating with the same awareness and so everything I suggest is just that, a suggestion. I'm but a student of life, and so I know what works for me and or what I've seen work for others, but only you know what works for you. Acceptance of what is, like the allowing meditation, works wonders for me. I can feel that when I am in resistance to what is, my anxiety amplifies, and then I automatically repress to band-aiding instead of processing and healing.

It's kind of like in *Monsters Inc.* – when you don't give the monsters your fear they don't have power. And so when I'm in acceptance of what is, not dismissing it but with an awareness that it only has the power over me that I allow it, I am able to gain a sense of clarity and control, to put it into perspective and act from that space.

Forgiveness
Oh, it's that word again. It can get thrown around so freely and be made to seem so simple. But what has held the most power for me is the perspective I get from these words:

> 'Forgiveness is the fragrance the violet sheds on the heel that has crushed it.'
>
> Mark Twain

And that includes our own heel. Because most frequently we are the ones holding ourselves hostage in unforgiveness, because we hold ourselves up to an ideal not created for or by us. We think we are supposed to be some sort of superhuman that makes all the right choices, says all the right things and never for a moment slips up, or live our lives by conditioning, stay in toxic relationships, buy things for our value or choose a career path for recognition.

Mistakes. I can't find a better word. I don't like that word, or the word 'failure' because I don't feel like there's such a thing.

I feel that every experience is an opportunity to learn. Some of us learn the first time around and some the tenth, but what does it matter when there's no judge except ourselves and so forgiveness begins with us.

We have to forgive ourselves for whatever perceived shortcomings or missteps we have made, whatever relationships we have stayed in for fear of letting go and falling, whatever jobs we stayed at for fear of looking small, and even for that closet full of clothes we can't bear to part with. We just need to take a deep breath and forgive ourself. Set ourself free and give ourself permission to do it on our own time in our way. It doesn't have to happen overnight.

Baby steps to big goals. It's more sustainable that way.

Clearing

What does clearing mean to you? What does it look like? Where are you? Are you in a quiet space clearing your mind or are you sitting in a room filled with old papers, pictures and clothes?

Are you sitting in front of your book keeper or accountant? Or at your desk with a consultant reviewing systems that work and systems that no longer work? Are you with your partner/husband/wife/spouse prioritizing your life?

Whatever looks like you in your current situation, you're clearing your current path to make way for a new path that works for you. It's a path that's more refined, easeful and in alignment with your intent or highest good.

It could be clearing old thoughts or patterns that don't work for you. Or literally clearing out papers that are no longer relevant, or pictures that trigger suffering, or clothes that are worn out or no longer fit and that are creating physical clutter which also contribute to mental clutter. This is the premise of the art of Feng Shui, to clear and organize your space in a manner that creates a Zen-like energy flow. You've probably seen or read articles titled 'Feng Shui Your Life', 'Feng Shui for Success' or 'Feng Shui for Better Health'. All with the intent of clearing your path for optimal energy flow. You might also have heard of the Marie Kondo art of tidying phenomenon, which encourages you to surround yourself only with what you need and what brings you joy.

Everything is energy, and so to have a clear space – whether it be our minds, our homes or our offices – is essential to our wellbeing and to being in alignment with our authentic selves.

'Out with the old, in with the true,' as my friend Jeff Brown says. Taking inventory of what's relevant, essential and what's true for you at any given moment or transition point. Clarifying what is blocking or causing suffering and clearing it from your path to make way for what serves to lift you higher.

Burning

The burning tradition or practice is something I learned through workshops and indigenous ceremonies. We would first begin with a round circle talk where we shared what was on our hearts and each offer our perspectives to those that shared in how we've broken through conditioning, got vulnerable with ourselves and others who've earned that space in our lives and begun the process of letting go and healing.

We would then write down on a piece of paper what we would like to be free from, take it to the fire and, one at a time, throw them in the fire to burn physically and metaphorically. We were welcome to share it aloud, or to let it silently burn.

I remember one of the first burning ceremonies I attended was on a journey I took with a company called The Divine Destination Collection to Muskoka, Ontario. We had a beautiful fall harvest dinner. After dinner our facilitator encouraged us to write down anything that we wanted to free ourselves from and bring it to the fire to burn.

The first word that came to me was faith. One would think it odd to want to rid yourself of faith but to me faith meant limitation. I had grown up with a family deeply engrained in the Christian faith, most predominantly on my father's Pentecostal side, and within that faith at the time who I am, and most of my actions and relations, were considered an abomination. So faith to me meant judgement, restriction and suffering and I wanted to free myself from that so that I could experience an openness to learn spirituality on my own terms with an open heart and mind. A deeply conditioned faith, even though I had walked away from it, was picking me up and putting me down like a puppet in everything I did in my life and inhibiting me from being able to experience my life fully and authentically.

There were many other times I participated in burning ceremonies – some indigenous some not, some on full moons and some spontaneously on my balcony. However, each time the act of physically writing down what I wanted to clear somehow brought to the surface something to be meditated on, brought to awareness, accepted, forgiven, cleared and finally let go and burned, making its way back into the place from which it came.

Reflection: What and When to Let Go

Letting go of what doesn't serve us is a process like everything in life. It takes great strength and courage to dig deep into our lives on whatever level and bring to awareness that which doesn't serve us to make room for what does.

Sometimes it's the end of a relationship, most recently many of my friends have ended their long-term relationships, some of 25 years, not because they had changed but they had finally awakened to the reality that their relationships didn't serve their highest good.

Over the past 20 years I have watched so many walk away from careers that no longer worked for them, sold cars that once held value but with a new relation to them just became the things that they were – four wheels and an engine that took them from a to b.

I've witnessed friends that were borderline hoarders Feng Shui their homes and their lives and experience joy, peace and the feeling of freedom that had eluded them their entire lives.

We've all been, or maybe even still are in subtle and not so subtle ways, prisoners holding on and bandaging ourselves with relationships, food, alcohol, drugs, work, cigarettes or whatever things we collect to cover our wounds. Out of sight, out of mind – right? Wrong … The only way to it is through it, and we will not heal the wounds of our past by holding on, but by bringing our awareness to them, healing and then letting go.

PART 2

IT'S JUST HERE TO MAKE YOU QUESTION – RESISTANCE

So you've begun to 'do the work' – you've taken the time to be in solitude in whatever form makes sense for you. You've worked through your conditioning, started to self-inquire and have uncovered the crystal beneath the dirt mirroring your truest, and most authentic, self. And now I hope you're intrigued.

Your awareness of yourself is becoming clearer. You've polished the mirror and are beginning to wake up to the fact that your strings were being pulled by others. You've looked around at your life and begun to take notice of what's not serving you and you're feeling called to keep digging, but there seems to be a force that's pulling you back.

Perhaps it feels like pressure in your head or confusion, shortness of breath or a rush of emotions. A fear arises and you may begin to mistrust; thoughts going through your mind such as 'this is not the time'. It might feel as if your heart's saying one thing and your head another. That could be conditioning, or your instinctive reptilian brain trying to protect you from what it feels is real danger. But most likely, especially in regards to choosing the path of authenticity, it's fear and conditioning. Perhaps it's a fear of looking inside and triggering emotions that have been suppressed, or that you will lose control, that everything will be different and it's going to take more work than you have the energy for. Or that it will create a ripple effect in your life for which you're not prepared.

This is what we call resistance. This force that strikes up against us, it seems, at every choice point – whether it's something as small as choosing a sandwich at our local café, or as large as changing our entire life's path. It begins to bring up emotions we perhaps didn't realize were there, fears we didn't know existed and voices that up until now we thought were our own. It's a force that many of us, on many occasions, have allowed to stop us dead in our tracks. Even if it meant going against our own intuition.

Why? Because it's really convincing. It's our mind playing on every thought, feeling and insecurity that it can to keep us 'safe'. It's remembered every voice we've heard – our mother's voice, our father's or teacher's voice and every lesson we've taken, every book we've read and event we've experienced. It's even been stored in our DNA from the collective experiences of our ancestors.

And just like our mothers, fathers, teachers and friends, at the heart of the matter it is there to protect us. Or so it thinks. But somewhere along the line our hearts seem to have disconnected from our heads. Our thinking mind became the master of our heart rather than our heart the master of our thinking mind.

CHAPTER 5

POLISHING THE MIRROR – RELATIONSHIPS

Connections are our opportunity to be ourselves, see ourselves and heal ourselves. They are our mirror to our inner world and can either suppress or expand us. We choose. Part of breaking through resistance is learning to listen, to pay attention to the whispers and to focus on building upon our relationships with those whose intentions are in alignment with our own.

They begin with our parents, grandparents, aunts, uncles and siblings, and then expand once we begin school to our teachers and peer group, as well as the people we meet along the way – from doctors and neighbours to janitors and our friends' parents. Everyone has the potential to impact who we are, who we'll become and our resistance to that – both positively and negatively.

Take yourself back to your first experience at school, or preschool if you started early. What did it look like? Who was there? And what impact did they have on you? Or even earlier – what is the first experience you can remember as a child? **We come into this world an impressionable being and everything in the path of our growth has an influence on who we are, who we become and the character that will define us, through both our trials and tribulations.**

Did your first interaction with a dog make you resistant towards animals, or your first interaction with a male figure make you wary of men? Was it an early interaction with a teacher that made you feel powerless or stupid? Each of those experiences has had an impact on the level of resistance you have. Maybe within you was the desire to become a veterinarian, but your fear of dogs held you back? Or your first interaction with men set the stage for your future relationships, and your teacher had an impact on how your entire educational journey would go?

As I sit here typing these words, I think of the teacher who told me I'd never be a writer and I know that her words had a powerful impact, and led to the resistance that keeps me from putting finger to key. Sometimes I sit here for hours, typing and erasing, typing and erasing, and then closing my laptop on an unproductive day. I've taken retreats to be inspired to write, walks with my dogs, meditations, made the environment just right with the perfect music, my favourite tea and the balcony door open letting in the cool breeze off the lake. But still nothing. And then finally I give myself permission to stop. I take the pressure off and say to myself, 'What if you never write again, how does that feel?' And it just doesn't feel right. I feel an intrinsic desire to express myself, my deepest emotions, my stories and the wisdom I've gained, both for self-reflection and in hope of inspiring others. So then why can't I just sit down and write? Or why can't you seem to have a healthy relationship? Or why can't you just walk up to that dog and pet him?

Resistance, that's why. Resistance is that habitual force that kicks up in us, especially it seems when we're ready to take action on something that's deeply authentic. In my case, that's writing. That voice comes again: 'You will never be a writer,' and because I saw that teacher as an authority in my life I gave her the power to choose for me. And so her voice became the resistance that shows up every time I sit down to write.

Even now at 40-odd years old, after a successful career in marketing, business development and events, as well as being the creator, producer and editor of one of the world's largest online personal development resources VividLife.me, resistance kicks up every time I embark on a new endeavor. And especially when that endeavor is calling me higher. Does this sound familiar? When you're called higher, maybe as a promotion at work or to take your relationship to the next level, that nagging voice is there waiting for you.

Each of these endeavors or experiences that prompts our resistance is a chance to polish the mirror – to look deep within ourselves, to pull out what's blocking us and have a look at it. When was it? Where was it? Who was it? Take a journey through your mind's eye back to the experience(s) that shaped you, back to the experience(s) that created the resistance standing between who you are and who you want to be.

We can apply this to every area of our lives and we can look into our relationships and connections past and present to find the keys to breaking through this resistance. Maybe you grew up with a bossy older sister and never found the courage to stand your ground, and that's mirrored in all of your relationships today. Or you were the youngest sibling and you always felt left out. Or you were the oldest and felt you had to take responsibility for everyone and everything, and just wanted to break free from responsibility altogether.

Take a look at how those connections within your life moulded who you are, and created the resistance to who you'd like to become, or who you really are. Maybe you latched on to the first partner that gave you attention, but now you're not feeling like this relationship is in alignment with who you really are. You might have children and have built a life together and be resistant to taking the leap for fear of what that will look like. Sometimes the friends that you grew up with just didn't seem to actually grow, and you're feeling called to build relationships that will help you grow, that take you higher. But there's that resistance thing again … coming to us in voices, in memories and in conditioned thoughts that can keep us hostage to a life that's not in authentic alignment.

So we keep putting on the mask and showing up to the masquerade.

We have to be very careful not to place blame on the experiences and the connections we've made within them. **Our life is our responsibility. Our karma is in our actions. We are responsible for every choice we make and the consequences for those choices.** An Oprah Winfrey quote comes to mind:

> Nobody but you is responsible for your life. It doesn't matter what your momma did. It doesn't matter what your daddy didn't do. You are responsible for your life. You are responsible for the energy that you create for yourself, and you're responsible for the energy you bring to others.

This is what I meant by 'our karma is in our actions'. And so when it comes to resistance and the experiences that create it, we are responsible for reaching in, having a look around and then pulling them out by their roots. So then we can eliminate what, or who, is blocking us from the life we were born to live.

My Story: 'No, this Way'

> Once you know your own voice you can't help but recognize when it's drowned out by others and creating the resistance to being fully present to who you are.

As I put my headset down on my desk I realized that it was one of the last times I would ever do that, at least as creator and producer of a personal development radio network. I was tired – exhausted really. For almost seven years I had been creating, producing and promoting other people's content, in what felt like my dharma (life purpose).

I can remember from being a little kid that I always thought I would be a producer or perhaps even an actor. Maybe in television, movies … I never really saw myself in radio, but it's where it all ended up. And when the idea came to me through a friend, as a means for amplifying my platform at the time, like many things, I jumped on it.

I had recently let go of a job in the corporate world that no longer felt like it served my highest good, or any good at all really besides money. It provided. It gave me the means to buy and do the things that I thought perhaps would make me feel worthy.

They didn't, and through the shows I produced I began to learn and remember that my worthiness was not an outside thing. And while I sat there at my desk, headset on and both producing and listening to each program, I would absorb the wisdom and feel a spiritual fire burning within my soul like nothing I've felt before. I felt invincible.

The shows started out with me both producing, hosting and co-hosting. However, I quickly took a back seat and began creating, producing and promoting the shows. My name went from headline to no line at all. But why was I so quick to withdraw my name?

That was a question I asked myself over and over again until a recent realization, but at the time I had no idea. I was convinced it was my life purpose. After all, from my earliest memory I remember getting all the kids together and writing and directing plays for our family. And yet from an early age I felt destined to be the star. I remember in middle school writing, directing and starring in a play about the effects of drug and alcohol abuse on the family. Back then I had no problem getting up in front of an audience. I mean I would have the butterflies, which is quite common, but the excitement would overrule any idea I had of withdrawing my role.

But somewhere along the way I started to resist the starring roles and instead faded into the background. From there a life-long struggle began, and my life took a series of twists and turns that would take me away from everything I loved, including myself. But why?

The problem was my relationships. My relationships started to become the focus of my life. I stopped giving my attention to myself and what was within me to give, and I started giving that attention to everyone else. Helping others has always been a part of my journey, and is still strongly with me today as I write these words, but this was beyond helping others. Every ounce of my being was focused on doing whatever I could to be liked. This became a main driver in my life, and created the resistance that would have me steer off course (if there's such thing) for a major part of my life.

I chose to take my life in the direction of doing for others before I cared for myself, of asking others before I asked myself. And quite frankly it ended that day when I put my headset on the desk. I didn't quite know why but a series of events, most poignantly a sharing group circle at one of my favourite places in the world, The Hive Centre, was the catalyst.

And it ended up being me – the person who created the program – who had a breakdown/breakthrough that day. Do you know those moments in life when things just hit you? You could have been told a million times, attended hundreds of workshops, been in therapy for years, but it just took one moment and one word to bring it all together for you, and then AHA! A ripple effect of awareness and understanding comes over you, and you can't help but do something about it.

Well, that was that day, at a group at The Hive Centre, not far from my home. I had this deep realization, and it was the catalyst to an understanding I carry with me today that helps me keep more in alignment with my most authentic self. The little boy in the director's chair, with the script in his hand, who jumped in at centre stage to steal the show.

I was ready to steal the show again – maybe steal is not the right word. More like I wanted to claim my role. Or better yet, to step into the truth of who I really am and give that to the world with conviction.

On that day, while others were talking and sharing what was in their hearts, I went into something of a trance and memory after memory flashed through my mind. Something like I've heard people say happens when you die. My whole life flashed before my eyes, but I didn't feel like I was dying. What I felt was that I was being released.

The memories came one by one: my English teacher saying I wouldn't be a writer, my friends saying I looked like a loser, my drama teacher failing me, my peers screaming 'fairy boy' at me while I ran with the ball during a soccer game, the cynical and angry voices of my peers envious of my progress.

One by one the memories came and with them were tears. I wept and wept and wept that day, right in front of a group that besides a few friends was mostly strangers. There I was centre stage, as vulnerable as I'd ever been, with everyone watching as tears flowed from my eyes. The pain left my heart and the reasons for my resistance to standing in my true power were revealed. There it was, playing like a movie in my mind: the faces, the relationships, the experiences that had held me hostage from my truest self for my entire life.

I had allowed them all in their own unique way to act as the resistance that stood between who I was and who I wanted to be. My friends were in my mind, picking out my clothes every time I got dressed, my teachers every time I thought about writing or stepping on stage, and my peers as I paid sharp attention to how I walked and talked.

All of these memories and many, many more came to the surface that day and, one by one, like thorns of resistance, I pulled them out and watched them heal. And with each moment I felt clearer and closer to hearing my own voice and having the confidence to speak it out.

***

I realized that I had been hiding – very well, I might add – behind the scenes of my own life and making everyone else the star, calling them all to be the greatest versions of themselves while I was allowing each of the thorns of resistance to keep me from being who I really was.

But that day I had the realization and the courage to be vulnerable enough. To stand, or in this case sit, centre stage and let it all out in an emotional performance deeply rooted in the truth of who I really am. And from that day forth I felt more free. Not that I wouldn't be challenged many more times; however, I now had the awareness to know when I was allowing my relationships to create resistance in my life. **Once you know your own voice you can't help but recognize when it's drowned out by others and creating the resistance to being fully present to who you are.**

And about the headphones. I see them hanging out of my old laptop bag from time to time, and once in a while I think about picking them up and I feel resistance playing its game – 'this way, no that way'. And then I remember, take a deep breath and put resistance in its place, check in with my highest self, and say, 'No, this is the way.'

The Practice of Relationships

Be Open

Contrary to our conditioned belief, being open with ourselves and others is crucial to a radically authentic life. It's not that you have to run down the street shouting out your story, but to share it with those who have earned it is in itself empowering. Obviously not every person we share our stories with has our best interest at heart, or sometimes they do at the time but as misunderstandings and the end of relationships would have it, they – for lack of a better phrase – 'stab us in the back'. And that's ok. Be open anyway, because to those who speak about others and share their secrets, it says more about them than it does about you.

It takes courage to open up and share the truth, and as Brene Brown says, 'Courage starts with showing up and letting ourselves be seen. … Because true belonging only happens when we present our authentic, imperfect selves to the world, our sense of belonging can never be greater than our level of self-acceptance.'

When I want to be more open, I try to 'tune in' to what I'm feeling and my intent, and break through the resistance to speaking up. Deep breathing can help if I find this difficult, but I try to act consciously to deliver my true self in my communication. If that isn't respected, then be strong and draw boundaries as you need.

And the more open we are the more connected we are to each other and ultimately to our higher selves. And ironically every aspect of our lives begins to align. We have higher self-worth, better friends, and are essentially happier, healthier and wealthier.

Ask Questions

Asking questions is very important in the quest to know ourselves, both of ourselves through deep self-inquiry and of others to identify their intent. To know the root of a situation is how we gain the power to fully understand it. And once we understand something or someone fully we can put that into context that makes sense on our path.

For instance, if we are constantly in conflict with, or triggered by, someone this is a great opportunity to ask questions. Both of them and of ourselves. For me it's an invitation to not just run away because I feel uncomfortable, but to dive in deeper to discover the roots. Because what I've learned through my experience is that it's not as I once thought, that everyone is out to get me. That in most cases it's quite the opposite, and never really much at all to do with me and more to do with how they are feeling, and/or perceiving me through the filters which they have collectively adopted to protect themselves.

Which takes me back to reading a chapter in *The Four Agreements* by Don Miguel Ruiz – 'Don't Take Anything Personally':

"Whatever happens around you, don't take it personally ... Nothing other people do is because of you. It is because of themselves. All people live in their own dream, in their own mind ... a different world from the one we live in. When we take something personally, we make the assumption that they know what is in our world, and we try to impose our world on their world.

Even when a situation seems so personal, even if others insult you directly, it has nothing to do with you ... the opinions they give are according to the agreements they have in their own minds ..."*

And this is a testament to why asking questions is so important to understanding others and ourselves and to knowing our authentic voice amongst the noise. And if I don't receive the answer that feels right, either from others, or through my own self-inquiry. I keep asking until I do.

'Be still and know.'

And eventually what resonates with your highest self will manifest. Either through your thoughts or your experiences, but what's most important is that we pay attention with mindful awareness.

Listen

One of the keys to a healthy relationship with others and ourselves is listening. And to listen with our full awareness. Where we are inspired, and where we are triggered. We can learn so much about ourselves through listening to others. **It is said that life, and our relationships, are constantly mirroring ourselves back to us and once we have the awareness to notice, we have an obligation to do something about it.**

Many of us are not very good listeners, we seem to wait to talk. Perhaps it's learned behaviour, or perhaps a protective

---

* From Don Miguel Ruiz, *The Four Agreements*. Amber-Allen Publishing, Incorporated (2018)

device; however, whatever the case, taking a moment to notice how effective we are at listening to others is a step in the right direction towards a deeper understanding of ourselves through others.

For example, you've just purchased a new house, or a car, or decided to take on a new entrepreneurial adventure and you are so overwhelmed with excitement you can't help but tell every person you come into contact with. And as quick as you are to share, as the feedback from others comes in you start to withdraw, feel resistance and second guess your decision(s).

Your mom says it's too expensive, your dad says that specific type of car is prone to accidents, and your sister says you shouldn't be taking those sorts of risks in your financial position. Each one of them projecting quite possibly their own fears, as well as mirroring back to you your own doubts and resistance.

But not in every case. In many cases the feedback you are receiving is educated through their own experience. And this is where a deep sense of listening and discernment comes in. Both taking a deep breath and listening to what the other has to say and then discerning whether or not their opinion rings true for yourself. Using every example, word and trigger to check in with yourself against your own voice.

It can get difficult to sort out all the voices in our heads. There's the crossing guard from elementary school, the drama teacher from high school, the bullies, the old boss, Mom, Dad, Sister, Brother. However, amongst each of those voices is our own and the quieter we become the more we can hear it."

Conscious Action vs. Reaction
And now this, conscious action versus reaction, has been my saving grace in many conflicts and triggering moments in my relationships. My conditioning, from witnessing relationships

---

" Quote attributed to Ram Dass

on my journey, would have me react when I'm triggered in any given situation, and from my experience, reacting causes war within and without every single time.

Our reactions to life, experiences, conflicts and triggers end up as projections of experiences and emotional trauma from our pasts not dealt with. Perhaps we are in a new relationship and our partner speaks words that are familiar from previous relationships, and we automatically react and project, which ends up creating the same relationship over and over again. Or we have a boss that questions us, or isn't quite all sunshine and rainbows about a project we hand in, which takes us back to an experience in high school, and we react from that experience versus responding to the current one.

This reminds me of an interview that I listened to on *Q* on CBC Radio here in Canada about a Whitney Houston documentary, and the fact that she had been sexually abused by a family member and how every experience going forward in her life was influenced by that experience, which ended up affecting her relationships with herself, others, and eventually leading to the addictions that took her life.

If we don't take the time to step back from our reactionary state to find the roots, and our truth within it, it can create a ripple effect of conflict both within and without, and can hold us hostage to an inauthentic existence without us ever being aware of it. We can begin to believe that we are the victim, or that the person in front of us, no matter who they are and what their actual intent, is the perpetrator of that pain, and then we project it on them. Whether they are responsible for it or not.

Conscious action requires us to take a step back, a deep breath, or even a few minutes, hours or days to do some deep reflection, self-inquiry, or meditation on why; to gain a greater understanding of ourselves, and to communicate clearly and compassionately from that perspective.

Reflection: Ask Questions, Listen and Respond

Wow, oh wow! Isn't it interesting how our relationships can be the key to our freedom in discovering our most authentic selves? And if we don't give ourselves the opportunity to open up and engage in them truthfully, vulnerably and with the understanding that we're all perfectly imperfect, they can also be what holds us hostage from truly knowing ourselves.

I know, and have met, many different people – unique personalities from all different walks of life – however, it seems that no matter where people come from there are very distinct personalities amongst them. There's the happy-go-lucky, the bad-tempered, the cool and collected, and the melancholic. Each personality is a collective of their genetic disposition and experiences, all interacting with each other; getting along, hitting triggers, causing conflicts, and projecting, but essentially all different points of difference and perspectives are opportunities to know ourselves and our voices better.

Whether it's a conflict with a spouse, a point of difference in politics, or a personal opinion about our choices, relationships can either be a point of resistance, or a mirror of opportunity into the truth of who we really are. And what sets them apart is our willingness to be open, ask questions, listen and respond with conscious action versus reaction.

CHAPTER 6

A WHOLE OTHER LEVEL – EVOLUTION

Have you ever wanted to experience life on a whole other level? Perhaps you were, or are, afraid of what that might look like? Concerned that it will require too much effort, that things will change and right now you seem quite comfortable. But the truth is, the only thing that is constant is change. And as the saying goes, we either 'let go or be dragged', right?

Do you feel it? Have you felt it – that intrinsic desire calling you higher?

That's personal evolution, development or growth. It's the path to a greater understanding of ourselves, others and our world and is a huge contributor to being able to move through resistance with ease.

Part of breaking through resistance is constantly evolving, not allowing yourself to stay static or step back into the patterns that kept you hostage. It's consistently putting yourself on the path that nourishes your own personal evolution – whether through writing, books, programs, travel or the people you surround yourself with.

Personal evolution is a key to radical authenticity and a catalyst to a happier life. **The more we know about ourselves, the more knowledge and confidence we have to act with true conviction in every area of our lives**. From our relationships to our work. If we prescribe to live our life in a bubble, or at a standstill, perhaps never really growing from that character we played in high school, then our experiences will keep showing up the same – somewhat of a *Groundhog Day* situation. Do you know that movie? If not, basically what happens is the same experience repeating over and over again.

I've experienced this in my relationships with people. And it's been challenging for me because I am a person whose intent is always to use my experiences to grow and evolve more. Whether it's through political points of difference or a difference in belief or perception, I always want to grow through it, and what I find the most effective tool is to be a good listener.

If we're not willing to grow, we're probably most likely not a good listener. But I can tell you from my experiences that not being a good listener, and not being open to growth, will stop you dead in your tracks and create an immense amount of suffering in your life, your relationships and your work.

Speaking of 'tracks', the whole 'peaked in high school or college' example comes to mind. I've been a part of so many friend and work circles of people who, like I've mentioned, still seem stuck at that time in their lives. They still have all the same friends, act in the same way and have never really pushed themselves outside their comfort zone. Perhaps they've changed locations – from school to college, from college to work – but nothing else changes, including them. They still seem to be wrapped up in a world where winning the 100-metre race, being on the soccer team, getting the house captain badge and having the right trainers (now the right house or car) and being looked at by the outside world as 'successful' are the driving force. Not their own personal evolution.

But they – we – have not chosen to evolve because of the resistance to what that looks like. We're afraid of change. We're fearful of our life not being as it's been for the last however many years and, most importantly, we are afraid of being seen as different – or worse, a failure.

There are so many examples of this in our current media, in films and television. Most recently I watched the controversial series on Netflix titled *13 Reasons Why* – a series about 13 tapes that a young high school girl, who took her own life, left for each person who'd affected her.

The series was eye-opening in so many ways. But most poignantly, at least for me personally, was the amplification of our fear to evolve for fear of how others will perceive us, ostracize us or even expel us from the group – our 'tribe'. So many of the characters struggled as they began to mirror who they really were, and yet they resisted their evolution through fear.

Each character was given the opportunity, through their own awareness, to evolve both personally and collectively, and to take action on that in a meaningful way. Some did, some didn't. However, what I found created the resistance for both those that did and the ones that didn't was the impact they felt it would have on them socially. They were all so focused on the collective thought that they didn't give merit to their own awareness and opportunity to evolve into who they really were.

Take a moment to take inventory of your life, both past and current, and ask yourself: where are you resisting your own evolution? Who is it? What is it? What experience or collective group of experiences has held you hostage from taking the reins to your own evolution and steering closer to who you really are?

In *13 Reasons Why* it was a fear of being ostracized or even worse. And in my own life there have been similar reasons – in school, college and throughout my career. I've felt the calling, I've heard the whispers several times in my life. But what held me back, what kept me from evolving, was always the voices of others which I'd allowed to become my own.

And it only takes one comment, one thought, to pose that resistance and to keep us static in a life that's not our own. It takes courage to stand up and become the person you were born to be. It takes courage to stand out from the crowd with the possibility of not being accepted. **It takes immense courage to begin the path of personal evolution, because what lies ahead is unknown and uncomfortable.** However, the only way to find yourself is to have the courage to challenge yourself, to plunge into the unknown, be comfortable with that and have the tenacity to stay the course through the trials and tribulations that will lead to the triumph of a radically authentic life.

My Story: I Only Had to Pay Attention

There I was, around 23 years old, sitting on the floor with print-outs of job postings from St John's, Newfoundland to Victoria, British Columbia – about a 7,500 km distance apart. I had finished college and completed a two-year course in Entertainment Administration, during which I'd had the opportunity to work with some pretty amazing people and companies producing events, concerts and working on world-class marketing and promotional efforts. One took me on a journey to Japan – my first trip ever – a 20-hour plane ride to Tokyo.

I seemed to be living the life. However, I still struggled with whether this was the life I was born to live, or one that I felt I needed to. After all, I didn't seem to be feeling or seeing any growth, personally or professionally. It seemed I spent most of my time doing admin work, and in my spare time working on pitching projects to my superiors that would hopefully take me to the next level.

The next level meant the corporate job, with the office, the view, the salary and lifestyle to match. I was searching for anything, any path that would lead me to that place, because, from what I had been educated to believe, that was where my happiness was.

But for the entire time I had an intrinsic desire to go out on my own and to build my own business, but I still wasn't sure what that was. I remember the day I applied for college. Browsing through my final choices, I filled out the application for both Entertainment Administration and Human Services Counsellor. There was a huge contrast between the paths I was drawn to take at the time – to work in the entertainment industry or to help people one-on-one as a counsellor.

I've always been drawn to helping people, even from some of my early memories. I remember at one of my very first dances (I was about ten), I just went up to the bar all proud to buy my own cherry coke. On my way back into the dance I saw a girl sitting on the stage crying. I sat down with her, gave her my cherry coke and spent the rest of the evening speaking to her about what was in her heart.

I also had a desire to work in entertainment, but never quite knew where. I loved theatre and musicals and acting, but remember being told at an early age by my drama teacher that it would be extremely difficult to get a job in the entertainment industry, despite the fact that I had already landed roles in theatre and was doing really well in class. That drama teacher also failed me.

Contrast and conflict had been creating a storm within me from as far as I can remember. As a child I listened a lot to adult conversations, and perhaps I shouldn't have, or wasn't quite ready. What I heard from them was that everything was hard: it was hard to get a job, it was hard to make a living, and it was an even harder road if you chose to go out on your own.

There's where the conditioning that created the resistance I would be up against later began. And it would only be fed by further interaction with adults, teachers, guidance counsellors, aunts, uncles and parents' friends. Perhaps it wasn't their intention to squash my dreams and make me afraid to grow up, but they did.

And as I looked at each job posting on the floor around me that day, all of their voices began to sound in my head, along with the ideas about success I had adopted along the way. At school it seemed to be drilled into our heads that without going to university we wouldn't have a chance, and that the most desirable careers were to be a doctor, lawyer or teacher. At one point I remember thinking they were my only options. Which is probably what led to me applying for college to become a counsellor.

And all this came flashing back to me many years later as I stood in a circle at a bush school near a village in South Africa where I was volunteering. It was the end of the week and each child that we had worked with was to state what they wanted to be. And there they were again, it seemed every young teenage voice said the same three choices that I experienced to be my only options at their age: doctor, lawyer, teacher. However, one brave little girl shouted out 'artist', and I was like 'Yeeesss, girl – yeeesss.' Just to hear that little girl shout out 'artist' in a group of people who had all chosen the same path felt like freedom to me.

She reminded me of myself at that age, but I had lacked the courage to break through the resistance I was surrounded by and shout it out. I wanted to be a producer, a director, a writer, an artist. I wanted to travel the world, and I wanted to use each of those skills to inspire people in whatever way I could.

But I swallowed those options deep within and opted to chase the ideal of success that had been dictated to me. After all, I was terrified to be ostracized, terrified to fail. And so instead of choosing to create my own path I decided it was safer to choose a path that had already been beaten.

And each posting that I looked at that day was a 'safe' option. And I was willing to go wherever that led me, just to get the corporate job – with the office, the view, and the salary and lifestyle to match. All the while fighting the screaming gypsy voice within to break free. To scream out, like that little girl in South Africa, 'I want to be an artist.' But I applied for the corporate jobs anyway. At that point in my life I didn't have the strength or courage to break free. It took all I could just to tread water, as I was dealing with a whole lot of baggage that I'd collected along the way.

Tears streamed down my face as I applied for each job that day. Not a moment went by that I didn't think about ripping up every last job posting, saying 'Fuck it', and setting out on my own journey – whatever that looked like.

But one by one I sent off the applications and awaited responses. Where would I end up? Who would hire me? There wasn't much time because I currently didn't have a job and was staying with my in-laws. So whatever came back, at that time, it was in my best interest to take.

The first company that responded to my application was a call centre in Kingston, Ontario about two hours east of where I was living. I jumped on it. The second answer was from a local newspaper in the same town. I jumped on that too. I didn't want either job. But money, and the traditional idea of success, were pulling my strings.

Both of those jobs would lead me to complete exhaustion, make me feel socially isolated as I lived hours from my family, and brought me to my knees with depression. I ended up leaving Kingston, but I took yet another corporate job, this time in sales. And I moved up quickly, from Sales to Director of Business Development.

Wow, oh wow! I was there! And everything unfolded as I was always told it would. I got the corporate job, the office, the money, the car … Everything started to look exactly as it was described, and for a while I felt I had arrived. Look at me, I thought – the kid from the ghetto, still a young man and successful.

But I still didn't feel happy. I felt an inner desire for more. I thought it was more success, more money, a bigger office and a more expensive car, but it was really my inner voice screaming for fulfillment from within. The voice that already knew what it wanted, the voice I heard the little girl in South Africa so confidently shout from. That voice.

But I couldn't let this go now. I had built a lifestyle around it. And when I stopped feeling fulfilled by my job, I started using the money to fulfill myself with other things. I started to throw party after party, supplying everything for everyone – food, alcohol, drugs. I was the 'It' guy. Everyone would come to my loft apartment, until it all started to spiral out of control and I went deeper and deeper into debt. All the while this voice was screaming to me, 'This is not your life!' Inside was a powerful desire to do good; however, outside I was doing damage. Damage that would end up costing me a lot of money, and almost myself in the end.

At this same time, my husband decided to take the leap and do what he had wanted to do his entire life: to open his own salon. Every day I would stop by his salon before work, during breaks, and after work. The excitement that filled the air as he stepped into his dream was contagious and a catalyst to me doing the same.

It was in that very place, as I sat behind the desk one day, that one of his clients handed a book to me called *The Four Agreements* by Don Miguel Ruiz and said, 'This book will change your life.' As I read each word, sometimes over and over again, I felt an awakening happening, a state of awareness and peace I had never felt before. The words in that book spoke directly to my heart and, word by word, chapter by chapter, I began to remember what it was all about. I began to remember the path I had wanted to take versus the one that was laid out for me. But I also gained a deep compassion for those who had laid it. As they were asleep as well.

It wasn't long after I read that book that I gained the courage to break through the resistance that held me. I handed in my resignation, claimed bankruptcy and began my own journey, off the beaten path.

One thing led to another. I started writing publicly about my journey, and at that time Facebook had just started and many others were resonating, so many that I ended up starting VividLife Radio, an online radio network to further my inquiries via conversations with authors and industry leaders. And from there, sponsored events and created a platform that reached millions – VividLife.me became a resource for written words and videos. Having hosted the likes of Arianna Huffington, Jane Fonda, Alanis Morissette, Oscar-winning actress Ellen Burstyn, Edgar Mitchell (the sixth person to walk on the moon), Peter Max (a 60s pop culture icon), as well as everyone who was anyone in the world of personal development.

I even attracted the attention of the biggest personal development guru and media mogul in history, Oprah Winfrey, who followed me on twitter. Wow, again I had worked my way from nothing to the top of an industry. Event organizers were asking me to speak and publishers were offering me book deals, but again there was that feeling. None of it seemed 'me'.

***

I had set out on a journey to find myself, only to return to the same role that was familiar to me. I thought I had set myself free but I was really still a slave to the conditioning of what success looked like, and still tied to the chains of resistance. I thought I had gained an awareness, but I was slowly returning to the trance of a life pulled by the strings of the collective. But this time there was no one really pulling the strings but myself, my own mind.

And what I began to realize, through a series of events, workshops, books, films and group discussions, was as Ram Dass says: 'we're all just walking each other home'. Every experience, every personal development event, workshop, book, inspirational film and group discussion was part of my personal evolution, providing me with the practical tools and wisdom to do the work.

And what I was resisting was that work. I was afraid of the work it took for the real transformation, afraid to use the tools and wisdom I had acquired for my own life, instead of producing the content to help others to find them. Like Dorothy in *The Wizard of Oz*, I had the power all along – I just had to realize it.

The Practice of Evolution

Daily Routine

One of the most influential practices in my own personal development has been a daily routine, more specifically getting up at the same time every day, opening the curtains to let the sunshine in, getting a glass of lemon water and scrolling through articles customized to my interests on an app called Flipboard, and, when I'm not struggling with laziness and procrastination, doing Yoga, Meditation and a walk in nature.

When I am consistent with this daily routine, I feel as if I am on fire. My mind is sharp, my body feels great and spiritually I feel I can take on anything. I'm more myself, quick-witted, and more apt to step out of my comfort zone to do things that help me grow.

I make lists, and goals that are in alignment with who I am, and am realistic in what I know I can accomplish. I work in baby steps. Baby steps to big dreams, as I like to say. But if I don't have it all mapped out, and haven't been on point with my daily routine, resistance rears its ugly head and has me lethargic and flat-out on the couch aimlessly flipping through Facebook, Instagram and Twitter, looking at how fabulous (fabulously calculated and staged) everyone else's life is, and then I can spiral into days of endless resistance.

So it's of utmost importance for my growth (not that we don't grow in our downtime) that I do my best to stick to a daily routine, with a manageable to-do list, with broken-down steps to reach the larger goals I've set for myself.

Here is a sample day:

6:00 AM: Wake up, open the curtains, do a neti pot (for nasal cleansing – I have really bad allergies and this helps clear my sinuses) and get a glass of lemon water (half a lemon squeezed in about a cup of water). I then sit in silence until I am finished drinking my lemon water.

6:30 AM: Scroll through Flipboard, stopping at and reading articles of interest; mostly on personal development, wellbeing, travel and, of course, food!

7:30 AM: If I'm a good boy and want to feel amazing in my body: Yoga. Since I took Yoga teacher training I usually design myself a sequence in alignment with what I feel I most need. Lately it is Yoga for sitting, because I have been sitting around way too much. And after Yoga I meditate for about 15 minutes, witnessing my thoughts and allowing them to vanish into a peaceful bliss, unless of course Oprah Winfrey and Deepak Chopra are running a Meditation Experience.

8:30 AM: I have tea with my husband until he leaves for work around 10 AM.

10:00 AM: Post on my social media pages, write reflections and blog distributed via my newsletter and website.

12:00 PM: Lunch, usually consisting of a smoothie, or avocado toast. Feed my dogs Mr Anderson and Mr Oliver and go for a walk (sometimes includes a stop at the beach).

1:00 PM: Depending if I've done Yoga and haven't binge eaten a box of cookies, I write, and/or work on business development.

3:00 PM: Tea time, or if I'm starving, I throw in a thin-crust pizza

4:00 PM: Complete any unfinished tasks. Clean up.

6:00 PM: Feed and take the dogs for a walk along the trail.

7:00 PM: Wind-down time: I usually watch a documentary or period film with a strong female lead on Netflix.

9:00 PM: Bed. I'm early to bed, early to rise. That is of course unless someone wants to invite me out for food or dancing, both trump sleep.

However, whatever it is that I/we do in a day, a routine that encompasses wholeness, a manageable to-do list and goals is of utmost importance to our personal development, mind, body and spirit.

Only you can know the essentials that form your best day, best routines, best needs, and part of creating your own routine will help you to understand and accept more of what you need in order to support yourself with care and respect.

Movement

Taking care of our physical body is also crucial to our personal development. When we're physically active and eating the right foods, our body is vibrating high. **And that most definitely creates a ripple effect in mind and spirit, making us feel optimistic to take on and grow from whatever life brings us.** I remember when my brother passed away suddenly that the effects of grief had such an enormous impact on my body. I felt like I could barely move, I was in constant pain, consistently having heart palpitations, and watched my blood pressure sky rocket to dangerous levels.

It's proof that our body speaks our mind. And so I returned to the Yoga mat, putting together a custom Yoga sequence for grief, anxiety and high blood pressure. If you are as emotionally sensitive as I am, and have ever lost someone really close to you, especially unexpectedly, you will know the physical effects on our body that we most often don't hear about. And if it hadn't been for a daily Yoga practice and getting out in nature, I am not sure I would have survived it.

Physical activity is so important to our wellbeing, wholeness, and most importantly to our own personal evolution. The more physically sound we are, the more prepared we are to take on challenges, and the more tenacity we have to make it to the finish line (and then start again).

Feeding the Mind

There is no personal development without feeding our minds. The world is full of so much wisdom, from those that have walked the path before us, from those still walking the path, from scientists, researchers, wanderlusters, entrepreneurs and industry experts, and with the internet being the biggest library in the world we don't even need to spend a dime (well, besides your internet bill), and if you don't have the internet (hey, don't laugh – it seems to be a trend in off-gridders to even get rid of the internet) you can head on down to your local library. And if you do have the budget and resources, Amazon is full of reading and now video material.

However, if sitting at home reading, whether a book or browsing the internet, isn't really your thing, and you have the budget, there are plenty of talks and workshops you can attend – from local talks at your book store, chamber of commerce or local networking groups, to larger conferences in big cities. I have been to many workshops, and taken lots of notes; however, I never really look back at them. I seem to retain what I need. But we're all different, right? Radically authentic, that is … So whatever works for you.

I also really enjoy browsing YouTube for inspirational and motivational videos, mostly from the late great Alan Watts and Osho, they speak on a level that captivates me. Check them out, and if they don't captivate you then keep searching for teachers who do. My husband really loves podcasts. Personally I don't have the attention span, I like short under ten-minute videos, but he loves to listen to Joe Rogan which fills his cup with the daily dose of intellectual wisdom he desires.

But like everything in life, and every practice, you get to choose what works for you, whether it's books, podcasts or videos, you choose what stimulated you the most.

Spiritual Fulfillment

This is a practice that often gets ignored. As a child I remember everyone going to church for their weekly spiritual fulfillment; however, it seems to be less and less as religion and spirituality have become private, political and more diverse in the West. Many of the Eastern teachings have made their way into and have influence in the West.

However, since I was a small child I have been captivated by spirituality and religion and they have been key in my personal development, and in the personal development of almost everyone I know. Whether you're Christian, Hindu, Jewish, Muslim, Wiccan or any other of the plethora of spiritual paths, spirituality and spiritual practices amplify growth. From my experience, all religions and spirituality practices seem to lead to the same place, kind of like the yellow brick road. So whether we're talking to God, Archangel Michael, Krishna, Allah or Govinda, we are really calling forth the highest vision and version of ourselves.

Community Connection

This one is so powerful as it's difficult to grow when you're in solitude all the time. We do require some solitude for self-reflection and inquiry; however, we are designed for and crave the connection of community, and what an incredible place to grow. There are so many people, so many groups from diverse backgrounds. It a virtual playground of opportunities to grow.

One of my personal favourites and one that I've written about my experience in in this book is group sharing circles. I have had so many profound shifts and transformations through these types of groups. I wouldn't be where and who I am today without them. They have also become a crucial part of my VividLife Group Journeys around the globe. As we sat around the fire in South Africa I listened to each group member share what was on their hearts, and sat back on occasion to watch how each group member shared, held space for and provided the wisdom that was the catalyst for almost every member of the group's realizations, growth and transformations. Their lives were shifting in higher perspective right in front of our eyes.

Another powerful community growth practice is mastermind groups: finding a group of topic-related people that get together frequently to share ideas and feedback. As each person shares a different background and perspective we get to learn things that we perhaps wouldn't or couldn't have learned through other personal growth modalities. And oftentimes our peers have had experiences that could in fact save us from a road of destruction, or amplify us on our paths.

One-on-one mentorship is also an excellent tool for personal development, both to hire an expert mentor and to be a mentor yourself; everyone is an expert at something and so why not teach what you know best and ask for assistance where you don't. If financially it's not an option to hire a mentor, which has been the case for me, utilize your skills with old-fashioned barter.

Like my mother always said, at least I think it was my mother, 'If there's a will, there's a way.' And community is a fast-track way to catapult our personal development. Creating just the right tribe is of utmost importance. **As the great Jim Rohn once said, 'You are the average of the five people you spend the most time with.'** So if you're not growing, look around, contemplate, and shuffle.

Reflection: Take a Deeper Look

Personal evolution doesn't need to look like attending a workshop or reading a book … however, they are good places to start. Personal evolution is really about paying attention, about listening and about using those tools and experiences to take a deeper look at yourself, to chip away at the conditioning and break through the resistance to being yourself.

Whether it's through our daily routine, movement, feeding our mind, spiritual fulfillment, community or a combination of all. What's most important is that we keep learning, keep growing and evolving into the highest version of ourselves, and to be in the awareness that the more we're moving and growing the less resistance we have, and the closer we are to being a living example of radical authenticity.

CHAPTER 7

WHAT WE PUT IN, WE GET OUT – NOURISHMENT

Food and our diets are one of life's biggest challenges, monopolized through diet programs which form a hugely lucrative industry. Everyone has a diet program that claims to be 'the one'. If you talk to a vegan they'd tell you that the vegan diet is the healthiest, they'll even back it up with science. However, if you speak to someone else about an alkaline diet, or another about a keto diet, they will all back up their programs with some kind of evidence.

But where does that evidence come from? Who were the scientists? From what corporation? What was the purpose of the study? How long was the study, and what were the varying factors?

Like many things in life, we are very quick to jump onboard the minute we hear that an authority of sorts endorsed something, whether we have actual proof that it works or not. This doesn't just apply to food and our diets, but also applies to our mental health and personal choices as well.

The bottom line is there is no fix-all, heal-all program. And there is no fix-all diet. Food and diets are individual, as is everything else in our life. We are born into a collective, but most arguably are individuals within that collective. Our individuality is noted from the moment we are born. Our parents begin to see the differences in our appearances and as we grow the differences in our character.

I was too lazy so didn't walk until after 12 months old, and my brother began to walk at nine months. I had blue eyes, he had brown. I was left-handed, he was right. I loved the arts and he loved sports. **And so from inception we are aware that yes, we are part of the human family, but that we are individuals within it. And so we should know there is no 'one-size fits all'.**

It seems the more we know about food, or at least the more food-related research that we have access to, the more suffering we have around food. And the more food becomes a psychological circus versus a physical need. And that psychological circus becomes the distraction which creates the resistance to pay attention to our own authentic needs.

How can we possibly hear our own voices when in the age of information we are so overwhelmed? It's kind of like a double-edged sword, because in many cases knowledge becomes power. However, when is the point when over-knowledge becomes our nemesis?

I love to read. Every morning when I get up I pick up my phone and click on an app where you put in your preferences and it feeds you articles according to those preferences. Obviously mine is stacked with personal development articles, travel and, until most recently, a lot about food and nutrition. So much so that I would have a headache after reading them all and come out completely confused. One article would state that fruit is good for you and the other would argue it's full of sugar, and that sugar is the enemy.

Do you remember in the 80s and 90s, and even into the millennium, that fat was a bad word, and all the programs that were designed around eliminating fat from our diets? Everything was fat-free, and what was mostly used to compensate for the lack of fat was sugar. And now, a few decades later, sugar is the bad word. And researchers have come to the conclusion that eliminating the fat and increasing the sugar amongst other substitutes actually led to more problems. But we were told that fat was bad for us. The authorities had all the research to back it up. And now, that's changed. But then what about the research that states that vegetarians live longer, healthier lives?

I'm confused, are you?

But what I'm not confused about – and I have learned from my own experience from being the worst eater that I knew, from being vegetarian to vegan, to eating a low-carb, high-fat diet – is that diets create rigidity, conformity and resistance to ourselves. We adopt the belief that if we choose the path that's seemed to work for someone else, maybe a large group of people, that it will work for us. That we'll have the happy, healthy life we see on the cover of the program: the white teeth, the six-pack, the perfect figure, and that we will live far beyond what's expected of those that don't adhere to the latest research or trends.

Is it all being sold to us by corporations? Conspiracy or truth? Who knows? But what I do know is that it's time to step back from all the hype and check in with ourselves, and to ask ourselves what it is that we like. What is it that makes us feel most alive?

What we put in our bodies affects what we get out of our bodies, and it all relates to our resistance and to the amount of physical and emotional energy we have to give to our radically authentic paths. After all, if we're on someone else's diet, just like emulating someone else's life, we're not in alignment with our own.

Part of breaking through the resistance to being our radical selves is to eat what we love, and love what we eat. To break free from the collective conditioned food trap and start out on our own path. Whatever that looks like. But what's most important is how you feel – because when we feel good we look good, and when we look good we feel better.

Grocery shopping used to be one of my favourite things to do. I loved to peruse the aisles picking things up that felt good to me, and then unpacking them and neatly putting them away in the fridge or the cupboard. I just loved holding fresh produce in my hand, or putting all the eggs away in my fancy container, pouring the milk into the glass pitcher while planning what I was going to make with it all.

However, grocery shopping has turned into a nightmare. I've somehow become a sort of militant food sergeant, and the grocery store, especially when I'm with my husband, is my war zone. What used to be a celebratory event has now turned into what feels more like an analytical science project.

Every item I or my husband go to pick up ends up with some deep discussion, and sometimes an argument, about how good or bad it is for us, whether it might lead to diabetes, heart disease or cancer. We can't even pick up a vegetable without wondering where it came from, how it was processed and where it was grown. The list of questions that pop into my head over picking out a carrot is enough to give you an anxiety attack! And it all stems from reading and listening to everyone else's perspective but our own.

Food has been a challenge for me, and many others, our entire lives. From my first memories of having to eat something or be sent to my room, or getting it shoved down my throat, to 'that's too expensive' and 'you can't eat that right now because it's for tomorrow night's dinner'. As a child this all felt very restricting, later developing into what would be a life-long struggle with food, not as nourishment but as the psychological battle that would see me vary from 90 pounds to 250 pounds as a grown adult.

Food, and our relationship to it, can make or break us when it comes to living our authentic lives. It can become the resistance that holds us hostage, or the catalyst to our freedom. We choose.

My Story: 'Two Cookies a Day'

From the time I can remember, food has been a challenge for me. As a child of a single mother it was an issue of lack, and as I matured and went out on my own I went overboard. When I entered college it was mostly fast food, and as I grew up it became somewhat of a health regime, especially as I spent a lot of my young adult years working in the health food industry.

But none the less, food usually took centre stage as it does in most of our lives. Food controlled me, and the effects of my diet on my health limited me; both with my self-image as I yo-yo'd in weight, and eventually developing acid reflux and irritable bowel syndrome.

Food can be so good, yet so bad. And it's ended up being one of my biggest challenges in the resistance to being who I truly am. I wasn't really the 90-pound almost-anorexic that ended up in the hospital, and I wasn't the portly executive that couldn't button up his jacket. I was somewhere in between. And until I learned to look at my relationship to food, I remained a hostage to chips, dips, doughnuts and my favourite: chocolate-chip and ginger cookies. I could eat an entire packet in one sitting, and they tasted good going in, but going out – well, I've got IBS so we'll leave it there.

One of my first memories of food is, I believe, from just after my parents separated. I was about seven years old and my dad was taking care of me at my home. He had made my brother Chris and I dinner and had put something on my plate I didn't remember ever eating before – beets. I remember eating all of my dinner but I left my beets as they were foreign to me, and then began to get up from the table. My father shouted, 'Where do you think you're going, you've not finished your dinner.' I looked over at my brother and sat down. 'You need to eat your beets,' said my father firmly. And obviously it wasn't something I had planned on doing. To cut a long story short, an argument broke out between my father and me, and if you had known my father then that was a recipe for destruction. I ended up, as many of us with baby boomer parents have, having to eat it whether I liked it or not.

Eat all your dinner or else – do you remember this?

I think it's some sort of passed-down discipline left over from after the war when there wasn't much to be had. But it seems to serve no purpose in a time when food is in abundance, or did it even then? But whatever the reason, that interaction with my father would shape my future relationship with food. From then on, unless I wanted it shoved down my throat, I would eat my beets and whatever else I was told to, beginning a life-long toxic relationship with food, and with anyone in authority.

I did what I was told. I surrendered to others dictating what was right for me versus listening to my own voice (taste and body). I feel that this day, amongst others, was the beginning of the challenge to have my own voice.

And not only was I to eat what I was told, but I was not allowed to eat what I wanted, both for reasons of discipline and finance. I remember going grocery shopping with my mother who would always do her best to buy us whatever kids' cereal she could. My favourites were called Count Chocula and Captain Crunch (which left the top of your mouth rough). I liked treats for our lunch like Wagon Wheels, or my absolute favourite, Ah Caramel.

But since my mom was on a very small budget, they were strictly for our lunches and would be put away or eventually hidden from us. But from time to time I would find them and end up eating the entire pack in one go. I would also drink all the milk and eat all the cheese slices – partly through the desire to have what I was 'forbidden' and to ease my emotional distress. I was a growing boy and, as you can see, my relationship with food was becoming very toxic. To a young boy and even a teenager this was very confusing, especially when I would venture over to my much wealthier friends' homes for dinner where everything seemed to be in abundance and they could have whatever they wanted.

And they had so many different kinds of cheese! Cheese would later – well, in all honesty, always – be my favourite thing. Just as I got older, the cheese got more diverse, as did my relationship to food. And I was always curious about other people's food as well. I grew up in a predominantly white neighbourhood and when someone of a different culture moved in, the first thing I would do is ask them if I could come to dinner.

I'm surprised I didn't become a chef (my brother did), as I would have had access to all the food I wanted, and probably have ended up over 200 pounds again. I remember the journey to me gaining the weight started when I got my first apartment. I went grocery shopping with my roommates, and I was like a kid in a candy store, and my cart looked like it too.

I was free. I was finally free to buy and eat what I wanted and there was no one to give me trouble. And so I ended up with a cart full of chips, dip, doughnuts, chocolate-chip cookies and meat. I seriously don't think there was one vegetable in that cart – well, maybe a potato, but definitely not a beet. Week after week I got bigger and bigger, until the point when I began to be uncomfortable in my body.

But what I found was that the more toxic my relationship was with food, the more toxic was the relationship I had with myself – my self-esteem was low and I began to feel a resistance to everything. I didn't even like shopping for clothes so I continued to wear the same thing over and over again. And the more I allowed food to control me, the further away I came from who I really was inside. Everything about me was covered in layers and layers of food that was stored as fat.

I felt ashamed of myself, and lacked the energy, motivation and drive that I once had. Food became the source of my resistance. Like a toxic relationship, it controlled every aspect of my being and kept me hostage to a life that wasn't mine.

Until that one day my roommate came home and told me that a new health food store was opening up in the area. At the time, I didn't have much education as to what that was, besides my grandmother taking me to the Christian health food store when I was a kid, and all I remember is that it smelled funny. But I knew it was healthy and I knew I wanted a drastic change.

Both she and I went and applied for jobs at the store, and I thought that because I was rather portly, they wouldn't hire me. But they did, and that began another story in my relationship with food. It became extreme actually. I went from filling my body with the most toxic food you could imagine to the sergeant-at-arms of what was good for me, and oh, I let everyone else know as well. A full swing in the pendulum which I believed would be the key to my freedom from food, but ended up being yet another distraction from the awareness of the deeper challenge I must face.

I ended up so over-educated about food that everything about making a decision to buy groceries or eat became a major point of stress for me and I ended up so skinny I looked ill. As I sat and ate my small, almost tasteless dinner, containing mostly vitamins and supplements, I felt yet another shift and I would continue to swing back and forth from extreme to extreme until I met my husband.

My husband had also struggled with food his entire life, just in different ways. It also became a resistance for him and distracted him from who he really was. When your entire life is controlled by your diet it's pretty hard to feel the truth of who you are. All of that is covered or smothered by food.

***

But at the time I met my husband he had found a healthier relationship with food: that I refer to this day as 'just a little bit' or, as my doctor most recently said, 'two cookies a day'. The philosophy is basically that you can have whatever you want, just in moderation. That you control the food instead of allowing it to control you. And that you give yourself the space, before you binge, to ask yourself what you're really eating for.

In my case it was for control. From a small child that control had been taken away from me and when I was old enough I took that control back, but in a toxic way. I was so focused on the fact that no one ever told me what to eat, that I lost focus on myself, and my health.

And the key to the shift in our relationship to food, to each other, or to our environment, is our awareness. Once we become aware of the root of our challenge or suffering, we have the opportunity to shift our behaviour to release us as its hostage, and allow us to walk towards the path of freedom.

And no path, even the path to freedom, is without its obstacles and setbacks. Sometimes the resistance shows up like a thief in the night, temporarily steals our awareness and has us right back where we began. But what's most important is that we get up in the morning and keep trying.

The Practice of Nourishment

Food Diary

Taking note of why, how, when and what we eat is so important when it comes to healing our relationship with food, and choosing what's authentically best for our physical and mental health.

Something I remember quite vividly growing up as a kid, and now as an adult, is visiting my doctor when I had allergy or digestive concerns and my doctor would always ask me to take note of what I was eating and what my reaction to it was. And so I am mindful of that and practice it even today.

Of course there are setbacks, when I eat the food (chips and dip and cookies) that immediately cause an uncomfortable reaction and then steer me off course. But 'fall down seven times, get up eight', right? And this is something that I practice in my life, not just with food, but with everything. Tomorrow's a new day and so I get back up and try it again. Mostly I do it mentally, but when our lives seem to be so full of mental chatter it's best to write these things down.

So perhaps you can begin with a food journal. Picking out journals is a favourite thing of mine, and though journaling hasn't been something I've done often, when I do it, especially with food, it's been hugely beneficial. It gives me insightful feedback on what I'm feeling, why I'm feeling it and how that affects the choices I'm making, and essentially how I feel in my body and mind in reaction to those choices.

I would start with a 21-day journal. This seems to be a good length of time to gauge our patterns, not just around food but around many things that affect our physical and mental wellbeing. But, like anything, don't get wrapped up in the length of time but focus on today – baby steps – and one day at a time.

Here is a good example of what you could include in a daily food journal:

What did you eat?

What time of day?

Why did you eat?

Where did it come from?

What were you feeling before eating?

Did you eat alone?

Did you enjoy it?

Were you hungry?

What were you feeling while eating?

Did you eat until you were full?

Were you satisfied?

Did you eat slowly, moderately or fast?

What did you feel after you ate?

Record your results in as much detail as you possibly can, and make sure you are consistent but most importantly radically authentic in your answers. Once you have 21 days filled out, give yourself the time and space to review and possibly, if you're comfortable, give it to your most brutally honest friend to review as well. Those are my favourite people, the ones that tell you what you need to hear versus what you want to hear. They really have your back.

While you (and possibly your friend) are reviewing your journal, look out for habits that have either a negative or positive impact on your wellbeing; for the negative habits take some time to look at them deeper, ultimately doing your best to uncover their roots, and then reflecting on what you've learned, and what your actions to correct the behaviour could be. For the habits that have a positive effect on your wellbeing, find a way to emulate those experiences and incorporate more into your life.

Ultimately you will be able to write your own food story – what you've learned through your 21-day journal, which habits you want to change, which habits you wish to expand on, and then create an action plan going forward to focus on creating your most authentic food story.

Listen to Your Body

Listening, as has been repeated over and over again, both by myself and numerous experts from areas of popular science, psychology and personal development, is key to success in all areas of our lives. It is no different when it comes to our food, why we're eating it, how we feel before, and how we feel after.

Paying attention to every nuance and heed their call. Is your stomach grumbling, are you low energy, or feeling light-headed? It's probably time to eat, and you probably shouldn't have let your body go that far before nourishing it. This is when we tend to make decisions we pay for later – kind of like pent-up emotions only becoming a challenge later, causing further suffering both physically and mentally.

Also pay attention to how you're feeling emotionally. Are you upset, angry, bored? Probably it's not the best time to eat then, as I know when I eat in this state I usually go for the carbs like chips, cookies, candy. These provide a temporary high and then a crash that lasts much longer and ends up training our bodies to crave, and create, addictions around food. The more we have the more we want.

So pay attention and bring your awareness to your body both before and after you eat. **Our bodies are constantly communicating, giving us the cues we need in order to make the right decisions for our physical and mental wellbeing, long before they become chronic and life-**

threatening ailments. If your body and mind feel lethargic after eating you should probably eliminate whatever it was that caused that from your diet. If your body feels vibrant and alive you should probably add more.

But what's most important is that we pay attention. That we listen to our body and do our best to nourish it. And as we change, grow and age so does our body and what it needs. What once gave us fuel can drain us, and vice versa. I remember my grandmother always saying to me that when I'm older my diet will completely change, and I used to laugh at her, saying, 'I'll never eat vegetables.' And well, she was right. As we age, our bodies lose their ability to be able to process carbs in the same way and so they tend to slow us down rather than give us the energy we need to thrive. So listen to your grandmother and, most importantly, listen to your body.

Food as Self-Care

Eating begins with shopping. I suggest you don't go hungry to the grocery store, because you'll end up throwing the idea of food as self-care right out of the window. All you'll be thinking of (well, not really thinking at all) is carbs, carbs, carbs. Your grocery cart will look more like a teenager grocery shopping for the first time rather than an action plan for your healthiest and most authentic self.

Eating with intention is the key to food as self-care. What's your intention? How do you want to look and feel? That's your first priority when it comes to pre-planning your grocery store visit for self-care. Think of it as visiting a spa for your body. You wouldn't buy a skin cream that dried out your face, or a shampoo that knotted your hair. So take the same care when planning what you'll put in your grocery cart. Make sure it is full with goodness that makes your body and mind feel 'high vibe'. The higher vibe we're feeling, the more in alignment with ourself we are.

One of the best and simplest of tips I've ever received when it comes to grocery shopping is to shop around the outside aisles and areas of the store – that's usually where the goodness seems to live: fresh, local organic vegetables, fruit and other unprocessed nourishing foods. Once we wander into the middle of the store we run into soda, chips and processed foods that wear us down. So, as tempting as it might be, do your best to stay away from the middle of the store. Or if you live in a warmer climate you could eliminate grocery stores altogether by visiting local markets. In a colder climate, try shopping at your local whole foods or health shop, both tend to carry the foods your body loves. But remember, just because it's trending, and just because it's at the health food store, doesn't mean it's always good for your body. We're individuals and so it's our responsibility to check in with our bodies to make sure it's right for us.

And remember once you get home from the store that the relationship between food and self-care doesn't end there, it continues in the way we prepare our food, and how we spend our time eating. One of the most important factors in the process is our energy when we are consuming. And far too often we're not in a good space. We're distracted by working lunches, reading, watching YouTube, talking on the phone, standing up or driving. All things that contribute to mindless eating and affect our minds and bodies in a myriad of negative ways. Eating each meal at a scheduled time, with intention, without distractions, and chewing our food slowly and mindfully is the best thing we can do for our wellbeing. And the more optimal our bodies, the more optimal our mind, and the sharper we are at identifying when things are out of alignment.

Healthy Eating Environment
There is so much research that backs the fact that 'the family (or friends) that eat together, stay together'. And even more research that suggests that eating together is not only good for our relationships, but our health and happiness as well.

We have a lot to learn from the Italians and Indians, who for centuries have made food the focus of connection and home. Cooking together and eating together provides an opportunity to deepen our relationships, increase our sense of belonging, bring about laughter (the best medicine) and pass down cultural traditions. It also lessens our chance of eating too much of the wrong things. Research shows that if we eat things that aren't the best for us, it's usually when we're alone. And that when we eat together we most often have a sense of gratitude, as we know who's prepared our meal and can directly show our appreciation. During family or group meals we are most often likely to cook local, healthier homemade food, and broaden our horizons by trying new things (with food as personal growth).

It's much easier for our mind to find the point of gratitude if the meat came from the local butcher, the bread from a bakery, the vegetables from our garden and when the meal is prepared by someone we know. **And gratitude is a pillar not only to our relationship with food, but our relationship with the entire universe.**

Take a look around. Scan your food diary. Where are you when you eat? Who are you with? And perhaps, now that you know how important our environment is to nourishing our bodies, make more of an effort to get together with family and friends to make your meal an opportunity to create a deeper connection to your food, others and yourself.

Reflection: What's Your Food Story?

Food takes centre stage in our lives. It's what's required to keep us alive. And how alive we feel is directly related to what we put in our bodies. High-quality, local organic food prepared at home with our family or friends is the optimal food story, but it's not done frequently enough for most of us, who in the pursuit of a modern life of more have disconnected from the very practices that fill our cup. And without a full cup we really don't have much to give.

Besides the fact that we seem to have less and less time for presence when it comes to food, perhaps we've also adopted negative patterns around it. Maybe we didn't come from a family where we ate together at a dinner table, but all took our food and ate it in front of the TV. Or maybe we grew up poor and food was always a trigger. Or we learned that food was a quick fix for suppressing our emotions.

Whatever the case, food has an enormous impact on our lives and is absolutely related to our wellbeing. And our wellbeing directly relates to our level of motivation, inspiration and finding the courage to be ourselves.

As that portly executive who used food to suppress emotions, it limited my positive sense of self and held me back from going after what I wanted. And the healthier my relationship with food, the healthier became my relationship with myself and others. My energy levels, self-esteem, motivation and inspiration increased as I began to uncover the roots of my relationship with food, mindfully address them with conscious action and take control over writing my best food story. Bringing awareness to my patterns, listening to my body, utilizing it as a source of self-care, and making a conscious effort to eat with others more often are where I aim now. There have been setbacks, many really, but what's been most helpful is being kind to myself, mindful of my triggers, and then taking positive action in creating the food story that works for me.

CHAPTER 8

PERPETUAL FIVE-YEAR-OLD – PLAY

It seems our lives are becoming more work and less play.
Even our play time has become inundated with work, as we
carry our cell phones wherever we go and the traditional 9–5
working culture disappears. And even if we're not momentarily
checking our emails or text messages, we become distracted
from being present for play by making it all about capturing
the moment for our followers on social media.

I can deeply relate to this as I have my phone with me
wherever I go. Whether out on a walk with my dogs along
the beach or sitting on a patio having a drink and soaking up
the sun, I always have my phone right beside me, ready to
click on a special view or event, and most of the time I spend
so much time trying to capture it that I myself miss the
moment completely.

Sound familiar?

It's seems we've become so wrapped up in a culture of work,
work, work, share, share, share – that we have become defined
more and more through what we do and the number of likes,
shares and followers we get via social media than by who we
truly are. So much so that it seems every day when I log on to
any platform there are countless ads for webinars, workshops
and online courses to improve my social media game.

If it wasn't bad enough that we've given ourselves limited,
or no, play time at all due to work, we have now handed our

leisure time to online interactions. We engage less and less in person and make our experiences about capturing the best photo so we can share it with our followers.

On social media, of course, everyone seems to be living a playful, happy and wealthy life. But is this reality? Of course not. I have friends from celebrities and millionaires to stay-at-home parents, and what I know to be true is that each one of them has become increasingly more attached to social media. With the common conversation being about how many followers you have, have you seen what so-and-so posted, my traffic has dropped, all the while sitting together with our faces in our phones.

Sitting being the key, except when we're standing for selfies. We have become immersed in sedentary lives that lack a sense of playfulness. **We've forgotten how much fun and joy we get from being playful, and actually being fully engaged in it.** And how engaging in active play, and being fully present to this, has so many benefits to our mind, body and spirit. **Playfulness can be the catalyst that helps us break through resistance, releases negative energy and draws us closer to our truest selves**.

Our lives have become mundane and resistant because we keep on repeating the same actions, and we're comfortable there. It works, it's what we're used to, it keeps us safe. But switching things up, embracing our inner five-year-old and being playful helps us break through the mundane and activates a force within us that can break through any form of resistance.

There is actually research (like we need it) to back up that play reduces anxiety, helps develop crucial life skills, helps us become more focused, makes us better team players, has ample benefits for our mental and physical health, increases our capacity to understand and retain information and, most of all, is fun.

When was the last time you engaged in active, present playfulness? Without your phone?

When was the last time you kicked a ball around, or played with your dog, engaged in a tickle fest, had a day with the girls (or boys), took up a new hobby, got that old water gun out of the closet and chased your partner or friends around, laughing until you peed?

Do you remember? Was it today, yesterday, or weeks or even months ago?

I know I can go long periods of time without play in my life, and most recently I've had a very sobering experience that's shown me how short our life can be. And that waiting to play because I'm so wrapped up in 'doing' and forget about 'being' might never happen.

One of the most poignant examples of a playful human being was my younger brother and only sibling, Chris. His life was dedicated to living it up, not taking things too seriously, and making time for play whenever he could. He was always inviting me to BBQs, swimming, camping, fishing – you name it, he was doing it, and taking whoever he could along for the ride.

And through his contagious, perpetual five-year-old self, play became his legacy. My brother passed away suddenly at only 38 years old, leaving my mother, step-father, father, his wife Amanda and his three children, Brianna (20), Nathan (16) and Mariah (11). And my only regret is that I didn't take him up on his offers. As I write to you now I am in tears remembering all the invitations he sent me, and each time I declined because I was too busy.

I was so busy trying to build a life that I was letting the one that was in front of me pass me by. Too serious for play, I passed up on my own opportunity to infuse my life with more joy, to let go of my attachment to proving my worthiness through how much I could accomplish, and my opportunity to take off my shirt and cannonball into the pool and enjoy life in the present with my brother. Not only that, but in doing so I passed up on the opportunities that would have created memories that I could have cherished today.

I don't have many regrets in my life, if any (besides this one). I am of the belief that everything that happened to me happened through me, and is, if I am aware enough, an opportunity for growth. Play is the most important of them all, and I missed out on that opportunity with my brother. **However, through this experience I have learned one of life's most valuable lessons: to stop putting off till tomorrow what you have the opportunity to do today.** Because there may never be a tomorrow. And to be reminded of the importance play has in our lives, not just as children but as adults, because in reality we may be in bigger bodies and with more serious lives, but we are never too far from that little five-year-old who's always waiting to come out and play.

And in that space, when we're running and diving in the pool, kicking the ball around, playing with our dog, or running around the yard (or in the house if you want to get in trouble) with water guns, we are free from the resistance that holds us hostage, completely present and engaged, and radiating our most radical authentic selves.

My Story: Captain of the Jungle Gym

I remember running through the field by the lake, so excited to jump up on that jungle gym and take my place as captain of the ship. My playful imagination ran wild, sailing me from Canada to Africa to Australia and all over the world. Closing my eyes and imagining the people I would meet, and of course the food, I would imagine myself stopping for picnics, meeting new friends and just soaking up every little bit that my life as captain of my destiny had to offer.

And when I opened my eyes reality would set in. I would have to run home for dinner. The clouds would cover and darkness set in. As I opened the door to our row townhouse in what we called 'the ghetto' the reality of life – not as captain of my destiny sailing the world – but as the seven-year-old son of a single mother trying to survive with two young boys.

Our food was limited and our experiences confined to that of whatever little amount my mother collected from the government to survive. And it was there in that place that it all began – my desire to rise up, to do better and to be better, and the jungle gym that was my dream boat to a better life. Not just for myself, but for my mother and little brother.

At the time my parents had recently separated, and my father was seeing another woman. However, he wasn't around much. And I can remember my brother and I would spend long nights lying on the floor with our baggage waiting for him to arrive.

And when he did come, just like my brother he was full of life and playfulness. We would go tobogganing and ice fishing in the winter (although they weren't my favourite things, I did them to be with him) and to carnivals and fishing in the summer. My dad was the best at carnivals, always winning; and he kicked ass at fishing too. My brother followed in his footsteps.

As I grew, though, the visits with my dad became fewer and life became darker as my father struggled with his own demons eventually leading him down the path of addiction, and my mother with the challenge of being a young woman raising two boys. Progressively the playfulness turned to isolation, the isolation to insecurity, and the insecurity birthed a desire to be seen at whatever cost.

It started with a lack of attention at school and quickly turned to taking the stage as the class clown. I would do whatever I could to get the attention I was lacking, and most often I ended up with my nose against the wall in the hallway, or even worse sitting under my teacher's desk facing the classroom on picture day.

What I didn't understand then, that I do now, is that I was projecting my inner pain into the outer world. A pattern that would create many challenges in my life as a child, teenager and young adult. As a young adult the desire to be seen, the desire to do and be better, took form as a desire to leave the 'ghetto' and be successful and seen in the world. At first I tried to take what seemed to be the easy road. I signed up for the theatre at my school and began auditioning. At that time I thought that becoming an actor would not only get me out of the 'ghetto' and make me wealthy, but that I would finally be seen. I ended up as an extra in a bunch of plays, and so it seemed as if my fast track out, through fame, wasn't as fast and easy as I thought it would be. And through a series of unfortunate events – being severely ostracized and bullied in high school, and witnessing the deterioration of my father through drug addiction – in amongst the normal stresses of a teenage life, I tried to take my own life.

My life was literally no longer play. It took a serious turn of events that would lead me from the psych ward to experimenting with drugs and alcohol. All of these, as I am aware now, as methods of suppressing the past that had taken away my playfulness and created the pain.

I became more playful through drugs, alcohol and parties. Actually I became so playful I was the life of the party. Even the local taxi company knew when they dropped off at my apartment, 'that's the party house'.

And then I had the new and amazing influence in my life that I had fallen in love with, and am married to today. My husband Timm came along and whisked me off my feet to what I thought was a better life, the life I had always dreamed of, the life that would free me from the 'ghetto' and give me the means to take care of myself and everyone I could.

And so I put down the party crown in pursuit of reclaiming my role as captain of my destiny. I finished college, I got a job, and another, and another. I climbed the ladder, putting everything I had into becoming a success; and the more I focused on success, the more I left the playfulness behind. I began to become boring, and would go through periods of regret where I would become the life of the party again. I struggled back and forth so much, but eventually settled into the boring life, desperately chasing the idea of success that I thought would bring me what I so deeply desired.

Literally in pain almost every minute of the day and far away from that playful, imaginative kid who would run through the field by the lake, so excited to jump up on that jungle gym and take my place as captain of the ship. I wasn't captain of any ship, least of all mine. I was becoming a slave to success. At this point I wasn't even a slave to the corporation. I was running my own ship, but taking it in the wrong direction. At least the wrong direction for me.

I was repeating the life I'd seen of other successful men, but never realizing I was losing myself, my relationship, and my family along the way. 'Busy' was my excuse, and it was the truth. I would work from the time that I woke up till I eventually passed out on the couch beside my computer. My husband would just cover me up with a blanket and in the morning keep reminding me that the direction I was headed wasn't healthy. And that if I wanted to let it all go, he would support and love me unconditionally. That he wasn't in love with me for what I do, but for who I am.

He became a constant light in my life. Always guiding me to make the right decisions for me and always doing his best to entice me to play. Until finally one day the pain of remaining the same was worse than the fear of change. And I took him up on his offer. We ended up going out on a night on the town, meeting a few friends, and that event would be the catalyst to nurturing and expanding upon my desire to create more play in my life.

***

But life can't be all play and no work – or can it? I mean if you love your work (what you do) it certainly can be. And my mission from that day forth was to incorporate a little playfulness in whatever I did, and to start saying YES to playful experiences. And the amount of play joyfully expanded as I allowed it, as I learned to take life less seriously. Actually, I knew this all along. I had just decided to follow the path that I thought was mine, versus my own. My desire to overcome the 'ghetto', to be seen, took the place of captain and steered me in the direction of my ego's desire versus the playfulness of my imaginative explorer. Now I travel the globe, stopping for picnics, meeting new friends and soaking up every little bit that my life as captain of my destiny, has to offer.

The Practice of Play

Start the Day with Play

The way we start our day has a lot to do with how our day actually unfolds. Do we just go through the motions with a lack of energy and purpose or will we glide through the day with intention and joy? We get to choose. But what is most in alignment with our truest self is to do it with enthusiasm.

> 'The word enthusiasm comes from the Greek word "entheos", which means the God within. And the happiest, most interesting people are those who have found the secret of maintaining their enthusiasm, that God within.'
>
> Earl Nightingale

And the direct path to enthusiasm is playfulness. An innate force within us constantly calling us home to 'the God within'. **The more playful we are the deeper our connection to our authentic self.** Playfulness washes away the stress, boosts our mood and keeps us in open communication with our intuition. And the more in touch with our intuition we are, the more authentic our path and everything and everyone that crosses it.

But what's playful to me may not be playful to you. Playfulness to me is taking my dogs to the beach and watching my youngest play in the water and collect rocks, neatly lining them up along the shoreline; or channelling my inner five-year-old on the jungle gym as captain of my destiny; or taking a walk in nature barefoot with friends in the rain – running, laughing and splashing through brooks.

But what does playfulness look like to you? Is it being active in sports? Perhaps engaging in a game of squash? Is it joining a pole dancing or tap dancing class? Or taking a trip to your local pool (or the one in your back yard)? Whatever your idea of play is, incorporating that as a practice to start your day is key in channelling your best and most authentic life and brings with it copious benefits to your physical, mental and spiritual health. And the healthier you are, the more in alignment you are with your truest self.

Sing and Dance

Another of my late brother's favourite things to do – and it didn't matter where he was, whether the grocery store, the mall, or the doctor's office – was to just break out into spontaneous song and dance. It was something to be admired as he made it none of his business what other people thought, something we could all use a little bit more of in our lives.

I know I tend to dance like everybody's watching and it truly affects my ability to just break free. I know I've caught friends dancing in many situations: while vacuuming, in their cars, or down an empty aisle in the grocery store, and when they catch your eye they tend to go red and stop what they're doing in their tracks. You see, we suppress our natural desire to cut loose for fear of what other people think, when the truth is, we all want to let go. 'Now I gotta cut loose, Footloose, kick off the Sunday shoes.' Remember that song?

One of my favourite things to do is to sing out loud, sometimes just spontaneously singing lyrics of songs (or making up my own) that have to do with something I'm thinking or a conversation that I'm having. And it usually ends up in a fit of belly laughter, or once in a while an accident (yes – I've peed my pants laughing) and I hope to incorporate more of it in my life.

The benefits of dancing and singing far outweigh any negative reaction we might get while dancing around and singing with our broom (do you remember that scene from *Mrs Doubtfire*, one of my favourites?). They increase our vitality, improve our flexibility both physically and mentally, reduce stress, and invoke a deeper connection to ourselves and our environment.

So the next time you're feeling disconnected, stressed out, and low, put on Richard Simmons' 'Sweating to the Oldies' (I used to watch my grandmother do this at 5 in the morning). It's guaranteed to not only make you sweat, but give you the best possible start to your day, be a direct path to joy and keep you radically authentic. Ok, maybe 'Sweating to the Oldies' isn't for you. But we all have something that brings us home to ourselves, so find out what it is, and giver!

Get Creative
Creativity is one of the best forms of playfulness. Whether it's creating products for my husband and my bath and body company, planning our annual themed holiday soiree, picnic games for our birthaversary events, creating vision boards, making Malas (meditation beads), or doing one of my dear friend Elsii's 'Naturally Gifted' retreats where she partners connecting with nature and creating natural art – merging two of my absolute favourite forms of play into one, nature and creative art.

No matter what the creative medium, it's a direct path to stress relief, self-awareness, connection and growth. Creativity doesn't have to look like a Picasso. **We're born creative beings and each one of us is a unique expressionist.** For me my medium may be art and nature and for you it may be dance, music, drama, writing or photography. I'm open to and dabble in all of them. Some I struggle with, and some I thrive within. However, I find it best to keep open and keep exploring different mediums, as we never know what hidden talent we'll find. Diving into a Mala-making class, I found that I was able to create the most unique and spiritually powerful Malas which ended up being in high demand. And who knew

I had it in me to be an alchemist of scent using essential oils to create the fragrances for our company? What's most important is to remain open, never limiting ourselves to what we might channel from within, and where that might lead us. But whatever medium we choose, creativity is definitely a direct path to our most authentic selves.

Playdate

Waaa hooo! Playdates … so much fun! Whether getting together for brunch, dancing or a picnic at the beach, playdates are crucial to our authentic selves. After all, we crave connection, and learn more about ourselves from our relationships (mirrors) than we do from anything else.

Scheduling time to hang out or chill with our friends and families is of utmost importance to our wellbeing. Especially hanging out with children as children remind us of our innate inner five-year-old, and bring out our deepest sense of playfulness. Just being around children is contagious. They remind us of our own spontaneity, curiosity and sense of joyful presence, and help us cut through the resistance that keeps us hostage as uptight adults. I know just spending an afternoon with my nieces and nephew brings me home to myself and leaves me with a deep sense of inner peace that not even hours of Yoga and Meditation can achieve.

Recently a few friends and I decided to take a walk alongside the water and as we walked we saw so many families together – playing games, BBQing, laughing and swimming. Which reminded us all of our own sense of playfulness, and how as adults who've adopted such a serious 'all work and no play' regime, we are missing out on that intrinsic desire, and in the process suppressing our most authentic selves. So, remember when you're mapping out your schedule that it's important not only to include work-related duties, but to make sure you make a conscious effort to include as many playdates as possible – especially with those who lift you higher.

Reflection: Enjoy the Journey

Playfulness seems to have taken a back seat to our pursuit of success, when in reality it is crucial to our success. What I know for sure is that none of us are getting out of here alive and so our purpose is to enjoy the journey as much as possible.

There is no place we will get to that allows us the opportunity to play. There is no time when we get to cash in on the payoff but now. After all, we're the captain of our destiny and we get to decide where we sail. We get to say what, why, how, who and when. We are the architects of our own lives, how that looks, unfolds and what our days look like along the way.

And it's of utmost importance that we do our best to incorporate playfulness in our lives. The more playful we are the more alive we are, and the more alive we are the deeper our connection to ourselves. And success, at least to me, is knowing ourselves and doing our best to give that to the world with all we've got.

After all, we don't want to look back in regret, seeing, as I did, every opportunity we had to drop the act of being serious, focusing on what we thought was a 'success-driven' life and end up realizing we missed out on one of the greatest opportunities in our life.

Life is too short for that, my friend, and you are too valuable to sell yourself short. My brother was a shining example of what a radically authentic life, full of playfulness, looked like. No, he wasn't a millionaire – and yes, he had his fair share of trials and tribulations – but what is most important is that he glided through life and left a legacy of playful memories that have inspired us all to let go, break out of our rigid shells (the memory that comes to mind is a video of my brother running and jumping into a swimming pool that had just been closed), to not take ourselves and life so seriously, and enjoy the journey.

PART 3

RADICAL AUTHENTICITY – YOUR LIFE YOUR WAY

Whether we are aware or unaware of the conditioning that surrounds us – through our parents, teachers, employers and peers – or not, it is time to take a stand, before we spiral into a sort of collective disconnection, unconsciousness and depression. These wars within us are actually creating the wars on the outside. We struggle so hard with being human doings vs. human beings, and our discontentment and disconnection from our spirit (our highest selves) has gotten out of hand.

Our way out is in *Radical Authenticity*. We were born of something vast – out of this world, infinite, limitless and boundless – radically authentic, and it's time to return to that place individually and collectively. This journey to find Radical Authenticity is about undoing our conditioned selves, breaking through the resistance that follows, uncovering our highest selves and living from that space in our everyday lives, whether in the relationships we have, the careers we choose, the fitness classes we take or the food we eat. Remember that everything we do must be our personal choice – not something that has been handpicked by the collective, but an authentic experience we're drawn to from the depths of our soul.

CHAPTER 9

STOP MAKING MONEY AND START MAKING A DIFFERENCE – MONEY

Money, Money, Money … Moooooney!

It's seems all we hear about. Beginning as early as I can remember: fights about money, not having enough money, people with money are 'this and that', 'money is evil', 'money makes the world go round', 'without money you're nothing', 'we don't have enough money for that', 'that takes a lot of money', 'good luck with that – it costs a lot of money'.

Do you remember hearing things like this? Whether you grew up with lots of money or very little, money will have been a common, if not the most common, conversation. And so how could we not adopt the belief that it was of utmost importance? Not only to our survival but to our value in the world? And within that belief, our quest for more began. We've become a servant of money versus being of service to ourselves and humanity.

As we grow and as our social structure becomes what one would call more 'sophisticated', our inner value seems to become the servant of our perceived outer value. And so begins the quest for more, which never becomes enough. More money, more accolades, more things, more value. We sacrifice our highest good, our truest selves, our health and our relationships in an attempt to be seen ('valued').

But as we discussed earlier in Chapter 3: 'Your Worthiness is Not an Outside Thing', and with our increased awareness, we can eventually understand this. That is, if we're conscious enough to pay attention and realize that no matter how much or how little we have, our value doesn't budge. It's within, not without. We just need to be still enough to know.

But that's quite the challenge in a world that is so full of noise. Everywhere we turn we are fed the story that money equals value – on billboards, during commercials, on reality TV, in magazines, books, and especially through our social media.

How many 'get rich quick' advertisements have you seen while scrolling through Facebook, or while watching YouTube, and now via Twitter and Instagram? We just can't get away from the 'money equals value' story. That is, unless we consciously step away. And like any conditioned thought, or addiction, that's tough. Especially as the Silicon Valley folks are more and more focused on how to keep us engaged. It all reminds me so much of the series *Star Wars*: the Dark Side versus the Light Side of the Force. The Dark Side being our Ego, the Light our Spirit. It's a battle that has seemed intrinsic since our creation or the Big Bang, whatever you believe. As it is laid out in the Bible, as well as almost every piece of non-fiction, literature or childhood fairytale. We have opposing forces within us; our head leading us in one direction and our heart leading us in another.

And from my personal experience, our guts are literally the translator between the two. You've heard the term 'trust your gut', right? Well, I used to dismiss it as bullshit, new age jargon, until I experienced it within my own life. And when my gut is all out of sorts, I know it's a sign that my life is out of sorts. You see, from the time I was a little boy I had stomach and intestinal issues, and from what I have experienced, and from what I know to be true, it is because I was being sent signals that things were not right, or in alignment. At least for me. And once I started to heed its message, things began to calm both with my inner and outer wellness. Perhaps you're working in corporate finance but have always been called to be an artist. Every day you show up at the office and you feel lethargic, have indigestion, anxiety and just don't feel fully alive? I'm positive if you're reading this book, you have been getting signs, big signs, and perhaps weren't able to identify what they were. Maybe they're as subtle as indigestion, or perhaps as intense as anxiety or depression?

The key is listening to all the signs, heeding their messages, and giving yourself the space to inquire within for direction. That voice, the one that waits for us in the stillness, has all the secrets to our most radically authentic life. Therein lies the 'pot of gold' that the leprechaun is searching for at the end of the rainbow, or the 'home' that Dorothy in *The Wizard of Oz* went looking for, or the treasure the boy sought in Paulo Coelho's *The Alchemist*, which is definitely a book I would recommend if you struggle with finding your purpose or destiny.

And once you've heard the call, it most definitely doesn't mean it's going to get easier! This I know to be true. In my life, the closer I've come to truth, the more resistance I've experienced. And it shows up in a myriad of self-talk and self-defeating ways, like a trickster that seems to lure us back into old, unconscious patterns. This is where deep listening and inquiry come in. Pay attention, ask, and listen.

Every time in my life when I've felt the rise of these emotions and I've mustered up the courage to listen to my gut, to follow my heart, and to focus on making a difference and being of service, I get hit like a ton of bricks with the conditioning. It can show up as negative self-talk and other people's voices, and with resistance as fear, laziness, and even bouts of extreme anxiety attacks, and a downward spiral.

But I keep getting up. I've said this before and I'll say it over and over again – it's a Zen proverb – 'fall down seven times, get up eight'. The key is to be present to the process, it's all part of the journey to ourselves. Life is duality. We will have good days and bad, challenging months and effortless months, but what's most important is that we stay the course, that we cultivate the awareness to listen to our guts, follow our hearts and make the choices that align with who we are, with what our gifts are, and that we give them to the world with all we've got. And so it is that, when we are shining with authenticity, in alignment with our true selves, that is when we will find the riches (both money and other means) that align with our desires.

And to understand that in the powerful words of Marianne Williamson:

> Our deepest fear is not that we are inadequate. Our deepest fear is that we are powerful beyond measure. It is our light, not our darkness, that most frightens us. Your playing small does not serve the world. There is nothing enlightened about shrinking so that other people won't feel insecure around you. We are all meant to shine as children do ... it is in everyone. And as we let our own lights shine, we unconsciously give other people permission to do the same. As we are liberated from our own fear, our presence automatically liberates others.*

Do you get that? Do you feel it from the depths of your soul? Stop playing small. Let your light shine ... as I'm writing this I have the old Sunday school song in my head:

> This little light of mine, I'm gonna let it shine
> This little light of mine, I'm gonna let it shine
> This little light of mine, I'm gonna let it shine
> Let it shine, let it shine, let it shine!

Put this on your fridge, on your desk, program it into your phone and let this be your mantra. Let it shine! Let it shine! Let it shine!

The world needs you, but what's most important is that *you* need you.

---

*Marianne Williamson, A Return to Love: Reflections on the Principles of "A Course in Miracles"

My Story: On the Dance Floor with Daisy

It's a Sunday afternoon as I hear the bells of what I believe to be an ice cream truck in the distance. As its gets closer I know it has to be true, as I hear kids calling their parents and running from their houses towards the truck. It was pretty common to hear the bells and then the sounds of excited children no matter where you lived back then. And as I called out to my mom and my little brother and I ran towards the truck like our life depended on it, I was reminded of our limitations. Yes, I could have an ice cream, but it had to be under a certain price, and herein lies one of the stories that created my desire for money.

More money meant more choices and, later I would learn, more opportunities and attention. But what I didn't know then, that I know now, is discernment. Like any child would in the same circumstances, I learned that in order to have more I needed more. I would get a sinking feeling in my belly as I ate my Spacecicle and watched the children from across the road eat their more expensive ice cream. I didn't even know if it tasted better. All I knew was that I wanted it ... because I couldn't have it. And without the wisdom to know the difference I set out on a destructive journey that would lead to much financial turbulence in my life.

As I mentioned in Chapter 7: 'What We Put In, We Get Out', the very first time I went grocery shopping as a student on my own, with my very own money, I filled my cart with everything you could imagine. Everything I couldn't have, or that my family couldn't afford as I was growing up, and not only did that lead to my life-long struggle with weight, but with finances as well. A lack mentality led to over-compensation on every level – doing whatever, and spending whatever, in order to feel seen and fulfilled.

And so I did whatever it took to make that happen, whether it was delivering newspapers, cleaning out fish tanks, telemarketing, factory work, drag shows, working at whatever and for whoever would notice me, give me a job and money. I became somewhat of an employment chameleon. Never really taking the time to focus on what it was I truly desired but what would make me enough money to buy my way to importance.

I remember the day when it all began to feel different. I had signed up for co-operative education in high school, which was a credit program where you got to work within the community. I knew I was attracted to the program, but I didn't know where I wanted to work. I left it up to the facilitator to find me something. The memory is so vivid as I sit here typing: it was a bright, sunshiny day as I walked into the guidance office to meet the facilitator and as I sat down she said to me, 'Shayne, would you like to work helping seniors?' 'Old people?' I said. She laughed and replied, 'Yes.' At that moment something inside of me came alive, something that felt similar. The memory flashed through my mind of helping the little girl at the preteen dance when I was younger, and how connected and fulfilled I remembered feeling. The word 'helping' was what had sparked that memory, and the feeling of excitement that fired up my soul. 'Yes,' I said ...

And that would be the first of many endeavors that involved helping people. Both work- and volunteer-related. I remember how alive I felt just to know that what I was doing was making a difference. No matter what it was, if it brought a sense of joy to someone's life, it brought joy to mine. I remember holding spa days at the seniors' home, painting their nails and laughing. And one particular memory is of a woman named Daisy who said that when I walked in the room it was 'like a sunrise'. Then she asked me to dance, without knowing it was my absolute favourite thing to do – especially to old jazz and they had a plethora of options to choose from, from Nina Simone and Ella Fitzgerald to Billie Holliday. We danced the afternoon away. She was short with a button nose and bright blue eyes and wearing a cheery flowered dress. Her face was glowing and her smile was ear to ear, and I hold that memory in my heart today.

But it wasn't long before I felt that pull again, the pull to something that fulfilled (or at least so I thought) the desire in me to have and to be more, and so I left the memory of that blissful day in the past, only to embark upon a journey that filled my pockets and emptied my soul. It was off to college and a choice between taking a path that would help people but pay little, and a choice that promised fame and fortune.

I left my destiny of helping others on the dance floor with Daisy to join the factory that promised the product of my desires (more like my ego's desires). And I did monetarily well, especially for my age. My drive and ambition for more, partnered with a radically creative nature, worked in my favour. But this led to an emptiness and a thirst that couldn't be quenched with money. Because within me, and I believe within all of us, is an innate blueprint, a calling, our purpose, that no matter how strong our egos are can't be ignored. It's always right there, beneath the service, knocking on our heart's door, whispering 'here I am'.

And as fate (at least that's what I call it) would have it, there came a time when I couldn't drown out its voice. It seemed to get louder and louder and the more I ignored it the more pain I experienced, and eventually a bout of depression which began to affect every aspect of my life. And now, I had no choice but to listen.

There are choice points in our lives. I know them as feelings; sometimes they come as lethargy, anxiety, depression, and sometimes they come as inspiration. Either way I know them as signs that either it's time to let go of something, or time to walk towards something else. And each time I've heeded their voice I've ended up exactly where I was supposed to be – making a difference in the lives of others, and inherently within my own. Like Glinda said to Dorothy, 'You had the power all along, my dear.' And it was calling. I only had to listen.

***

But what was equally important was the journey. Each and every part of it: the good, the bad and the ugly. I wouldn't take any of it back, even for a moment. Every experience had walked me home to who I am. They challenged me, they opened me and they moulded me into who I am today. And without the challenges and the experiences, I wouldn't have learned the very lessons that uncovered the truth of who I am today, and led me to the understanding that my life, all our lives really, aren't about making money, but about making a difference. **And if we are in true alignment with who we really are, and using our gifts to make a difference in the world, the money will come. Because money is just a form of energy.** And the more in alignment we are, the more we gain.

The Practice of Money

What's Your Intent?

Everything, at least from my experience, revolves around *intent*. It seems to be the law of laws. The Universe, God, Source, Fate – whatever you choose to call the force that breathes life, it seems that it responds to our deepest intent, versus what we may unconsciously think we want, or desire.

So, what is your intent, your core intent? The purpose behind everything you do. Do you know? Take some time, get quiet and ask yourself. What is motivating my actions? Is it money, things, recognition, jealousy, envy, revenge? Or is it a deep desire to know yourself better, to find your gifts and to help others? Money, recognition, revenge – they're not rooted in the truth of who you are. They're egoic intentions. Conditioned and rooted inside us, these are intentions that perhaps are creating your suffering and the resistance to finding out the truest intent within the depths of your soul.

In order to get there you're going to have to start by identifying what's not yours and what's toxic, and then get stiller, go deeper and uncover what's at the core. What is it that you really desire? Sift through the thoughts that have run autopilot in your mind for so long and let them fall away, whoever's voices they are, whatever conditioning that arises, let that fall away too. The stiller you become the more you will hear, and the longer you are still and without distractions, the better you will get at hearing your own voice, and then taking action from that place.

And then do a life scan – a review of the times in your life that have felt good and those that have not. When things felt effortless, full of joy, what was your intent?

Throughout my life there have been many distractions that have held my intent hostage from being revealed. There's been so much jealousy, and envy which have taken the form of competition, which in reality is a distraction from walking our own path as we're paying too much attention to others to notice. This always reminds me of the childhood tale of the Hare and the Tortoise, which I use a lot when coaching others to walk their own path versus paying attention to others. If you're not familiar with it, the moral of the story is that when you focus on winning (competition), you lose every time, and when you focus on a life with intent, and surrender and enjoy the process, you win every time. It's not about winning against others; winning – at least to me – is about being the most radically authentic version of myself and then embodying that in everything I do.

Ask Around

Asking around may seem contrary to what I have suggested. When we are in a rut of unawareness it can sometimes, even through deep self-inquiry, be a challenge to hear our own voice. Conditioning runs so deep that even now I have to continually question if my actions are in alignment with my intent. And who better to ask than those who are closest to your heart. At least if you're in healthy relationships.

If you're not, it's probably not the best practice. But most of us have someone who knows what's in our hearts and can speak it when we have forgotten. Throughout my life I have had many toxic relationships in which I allowed their opinions to dictate who I was. However, I've found the more I've grown to know and love myself the more the people I surround myself with reflect that back to me. But beware, just because you know and love yourself doesn't mean the assholes don't slip in the back door. This is where discernment comes into play. **Pay attention – you know in your heart of hearts who you can trust. And once you have identified those people, your 'good vibe tribe', then ask away!**

Invite them in for a cup of tea, and if you don't drink tea or coffee, then a glass of wine, but not too many glasses of wine! Ask them how they see you, and if they were to give you one action word to describe your deepest intent, what it would be. And most likely, if they know you well, they'll nail it.

My go-to people are my husband, my mother, my mother-in-law and my dearest friends: Crystal-Lee, Raquel, Jodi, Elsii, Eloise, Brenda, Linda ... OMG, I'm just realizing how many amazingly authentic people I have attracted in my life. Most have seen me in my most vulnerable places, are deeply aware of themselves, and carry a laser-sharp pointer directed right at the truth within my heart.

One time I asked my mother-in-law, Marilyn, what she saw, and the perspective she gave me pointed right to what I needed to do to find the answer I was looking for. She told me, 'Your mind is like a mail room with a tiny door,' which brought me to the understanding that I have so much in there, so much wisdom and so much to say, but because the door is so tiny and I had never given myself the time to sort it out I operated in a state of fogginess. So what I needed to do was to get still and sort it all out, and well, once I did, like magic ... this book!

I've also found that those silly little Facebook quizzes work. You know – 'What Princess Are You?' or my favourite, 'What *Downton Abbey* Character Are You?' I wanted to be the Dowager Duchess, but I got Mary. Yes, I'm Mary. And the most intriguing thing is that once I paid more attention to her character, I realized this quiz was right. (And my husband got the Dowager.)

Fun and games aside, asking around is a great way to explore who we are, what our deepest desires and intent may be and then checking back in with our own truth barometer to see if it resonates.

What Would Your Seven-Year-Old Self Do?
This is a good one but also a deep one. From my own research and experience, seven years old seems to be a point of transition, when we stop listening to our own voice and start listening to others. Sometimes it's a challenge cutting through all the self-talk, conditioning and resistance to pull up a chair with your seven-year-old self. Also one that can be triggering and even traumatic. So if there's some dark stuff back there I would suggest a psychotherapist to assist you in working through it. I've suggested a psychotherapist, and not a life coach or spiritual teacher, because an untrained professional can only take us so far, and sometimes cause more damage. When we open that can of worms we most definitely want it to be with someone who knows something about how to take care of them. From my experience I've found life coaches and spiritual teachers to be great facilitators of philosophy, as well as to offer techniques and tools to enhance our path. But the real deep stuff, the stuff that when revealed can make or break us literally, I'd say to leave it to the trained professionals.

So with the help of a professional, or if you're able to get there on your own, get still and take a seat with your seven-year-old self. And like an Oprah Winfrey-style interview, ask yourself (your seven-year-old self) what he/she knows to be true? What's your deepest desire, intent, purpose, and what do you want to be when you grow up?

And listen …

Aligning with Your Passion and Desires
You probably know what you love to do – but perhaps can't see the bigger picture. You most likely know if you like apples or oranges better, so let's start with the little things:

What do you like to do most?

What makes you lose track of time?

What doesn't feel like work or effort?

What makes you feel fulfilled when you're finished?

I almost said 'a bag of chips and a hell of a good dip'. However, I know this is not true. It brings instant gratification but in the end, well, I've already said – let's just leave it there.

Do I like kale? No. I eat it because every damn article tells me that it's good for me. Do I like chips and dip, hell yeah, but it makes me feel like shit. So again, it's about going deeper, checking in with ourselves and really feeling for what's right. How do our food choices have anything to do with our deepest intent? Because it's not actually about the food, it's about the process – however, food just made a good example, especially for me.

So ask yourself, what are your deepest desires? What is it you want from life, and even deeper from what you do? Or if that's too difficult a place to start, what are you passionate about? Maybe exercise (make sure it's you and not you trying to look good for someone else), food, sports, arts, spirituality, making things, travelling or helping people? Write down everything you can think of, and if nothing comes to mind, then google a list of passions and write down those that call to you first.

Then look at your calendar and schedule in time in the next few weeks to focus on those things. Yes. Like an appointment, find time in your calendar to incorporate what you're most passionate about. I've found that what you're passionate about will most likely lead you to your purpose, and most definitely will teach you more about yourself and attract people into your life that are more in alignment. And, like magic, you just may unveil your gifts and your purpose.

Test it Out

If you were looking to buy a new car, you'd take it for a test drive. So let's apply this to every area of our lives. Not just purchasing cars. Once you have uncovered what you're attracted to, passionate about, or desire, then test it out. Perhaps take a course or sign up for a workshop, a team, an online group or volunteer.

I've found that in my experience testing things out has been super-beneficial and, man, have I tested a lot of things out. But I wouldn't take any of it back as it all gave me the wisdom and experience I needed to get where I am today. I'm one that follows what I'm curious about and if I don't I always feel regret, and regret is not a feeling I like. So absolutely no regrets for me – well, that's a bit of a lie, I have a lot of regrets around food, but I'm working on it. The signs are always there, the wisdom always speaking to me before I hit the drive-through … but we're all a work-in-progress and this is where I need it the most.

Maybe I'm a little too passionate about food, if that's even possible. But that aside, once you have a list of what you're passionate about (I'd start with ten) and inquire within to narrow it down to just three, and start with the first. For me I had a deep interest in theatre and so I volunteered at the local theatre and took whatever position they had. It ended up being make-up, which I knew nothing about, but I learned and the experience was fulfilling, and beyond that I met many beautiful people who I'm connected with today.

I've also taken many courses, workshops and even attended conferences around the globe. And doing so ended up in my exploring whether I wanted to do the same thing – run conferences, be a speaker or spiritual celebrity. I dabbled in all that, but through the experience realized it wasn't for me. But it did end up leading to the rediscovery of my ability to write, and use the media via my web series, My VividLife, as a catalyst to amplify my message of radical authenticity and, well, we know where that ended up.

Reflection: Who, What, Where … and How Much?
We have an obligation to use our deepest and most authentic gifts in service to the world and, most importantly, for ourselves. When we're disconnected from that we create a

ripple effect in the world. And a world out of harmony both within and without is a recipe for destruction. Imagine if I'm really an artist acting as an accountant then I'm taking away an accountant's job. We take away the opportunity for the right person to be in the right position when we are not true to ourself. We are responsible for our own as well as collective suffering if we are not in service of ourself, and using our gifts to service the world is part of a Vivid Life.

We follow what's trending, we do what we've been told, we choose from what's been presented to us as options versus checking in with ourselves and our truest intent to feel if it's right. We chase ideas of success for accolades and adoration. Falling short, and feeling empty within ourselves often using material things, relationships and substances to silence the voices, suppress the emotions, to shut it all out because perhaps it's all too difficult to hear.

And if we stop and listen, if we operate by way of our own internal GPS rather than the one that's been programmed for everyone, we may find that the life we're living and the desires that we have isn't really in alignment with who we are. Perhaps we've chosen it for fear of standing out, or perhaps we're standing out for the wrong reasons as well. But the only way we will ever know is if we give ourselves the space to explore, to evaluate where we've been, where we are, what got us here and if we're really on the path of our own choosing. If we take a closer look even at what we eat, wear, drive and who we're in a relationship with to see if it could have been a decision made from a place of conditioning and laziness, we can break through the conditioning and the challenges that follow to living a deeply authentic life.

And we get to choose. Just like in a restaurant (I know – food again) we get to choose what's on life's plate. But what's most important is that the decision is ours, we get to say where, what, with who and how much. **And if we compromise, we pay the price. Our karma is in our actions.**

CHAPTER 10

GRATITUDE FOR EVERYTHING – GRATITUDE

'Gratitude is the attitude', 'be grateful for all things', 'start the day with a grateful heart' … Everywhere we turn we see gratitude quotes, articles about gratitude journals and thankfulness prayers. It started with our training as kids and has worked its way into every practice, self-help blog, book and social media feed. But what does it even mean, or mean to you?

The dictionary defines gratitude as 'the quality of being thankful; readiness to show appreciation for and to return kindness'. And I get that, and I experience that to be true, but not as something that has come naturally but something that has to be cultivated or experienced.

As a child I remember getting gifts from my aunts, uncles and family friends and immediately my mother would tell me to say 'thank you'. But what did it mean? Why was I saying thank you, and most importantly why was I saying thank you for something when I didn't feel it, and in many cases didn't want what they were giving me (unless of course it was food!) And yes, I was truly grateful for food – I felt that with every ounce of my being. The rush of gratefulness intoxicated my body as a huge grin graced my face. I think that's when I began to understand and feel what gratitude was.

However, the gratitude that was forced upon me as an expectation from my elders didn't feel authentic to me. I mean, at five years old I didn't know what authentic meant, but I knew it didn't feel right to say 'thank you' when I didn't mean it. And so for me, and possibly yourself, we learned at an early age that gratitude was something that was expected, and so became another point of conditioning in our lives and like robots we went on aimlessly thanking people without perhaps even feeling it. And like anything authentic, if we don't feel it with every ounce of our being to be true then it's not, at least for us.

As I began to formally explore the path of personal development, every book, workshop and podcast would suggest a gratitude practice to start and end the day. They told me to start a gratitude journal. And a journal was something foreign to me. The only experience I'd ever had with journals was through my friends (girls) who called it a diary and kept it secret. I wasn't familiar with writing down my thoughts, or my appreciation (gratitude). As always, though, I was open to trying new things, and especially at that particular time of transition in my life. After all, the practice of gratitude promised me fulfillment.

So I purchased journal after journal, taking my time picking out the one with the best design, often costing me an arm and a leg, and I would write:

I'm grateful for …

But nothing. I couldn't feel anything. When I wrote the word on the paper I felt nothing and saw just words. I understood what they were associated with; however, I didn't actually 'feel' the feeling of gratitude. And what does it feel like anyway? It's described as an emotion or feeling in our bodies, like joy or sadness or anger. But all I had to relate it to was the feeling of getting food as a kid. And it wasn't something I forced, it was an automatic response.

Just like most of life's conditioning, I had no real connection to gratitude, and it most definitely didn't feel like me. It isn't like I'm some ungrateful human being, it's just that when I was thankful, it was radically authentic, from the heart and felt with my whole body. And I think my conditioning of what gratitude was caused my resistance to actually feeling it.

And so I practiced and practiced and realized that the journal thing just wasn't for me. Around that time I had read a few articles that said that journaling really isn't effective for men. True or not, I know for sure it was true for me and so onward I went to find a gratitude practice that worked for me.

Practice after practice failed to give me the experience that I was being told or had read about. Perhaps it was because I wasn't actually grateful, as life seemed to be constantly turbulent and the majority of my focus was on just trying to survive and to find my place in the world amongst the chaos.

But like everything in life, I kept on trying. Sometimes I tried a little too hard, causing me resentment. And the more resentment I felt, the further away from gratitude I became. But it made sense. How was I, or are you, if your life is or has been turbulent, able to be grateful for something that felt like nothing but struggle? It becomes all we focus on, and so I know the law of attraction says 'what you focus on you attract more of' and perhaps because I wasn't feeling gratitude I wasn't cultivating any experiences to be grateful for.

It's a challenging endeavor undoing conditioning. Some studies have said that it's even stored in our DNA. And so how do we undo that, how can we change our DNA? From my own experience I've learned that repeating the same action consistently creates a new pattern and new pathways in the brain, and so perhaps it could shift whatever deep conditioning that is embedded in our DNA as well.

And so, like any goals we have, we repeat and practice. I have that old saying playing over and over in my head: 'practice makes perfect'. (And although I don't believe in the idea of perfection, at least the one we're conditioned to believe in, I do believe we are perfectly imperfect.) I also believe that with practice, and especially a practice that's authentic to us and partnered with radical focus, we can cultivate newer and more progressive life-affirming habits.

Not everything comes naturally to everyone. It is an undoing of all you've been conditioned to believe, and a process of learning what gratitude meant to you as an individual. **Finding and accessing that emotion, perhaps that had been buried deep through life experience, is our opportunity to take on the responsibility of whether we allow the experience to take us down or lift us higher.**

Gratitude for someone who is in deep suffering could perhaps be a luxury, but if we can find the light of awareness to cultivate a gratitude practice that is authentic to us, it really is magical.

My Story: His Last Prayer

As I sit here writing my gratitude story it's almost seven months to the day from my brother's sudden death and a day away from an intimate gathering of my immediate family to spread my brother's ashes. I've been contemplating what I am going to write for the better part of this week and, as the day draws closer, an upheaval of emotions and physical sensations has set in. All need to be processed in order to heal and all are amplified at the intensity that I loved him, and still do.

What does this have to do with gratitude, you might ask?

It took my brother's death to teach me the most valuable lesson in gratitude. Not gratitude for the experience, as this would be one of the only experiences in my life I would wish to be different. If I had the power I would bring him back in a heartbeat. However, my brother in his life and perspective had little (in regards of material things) but was full of love and gratitude. He spent his life in the kind of presence we hear about in self-help books, and he never read one or attended a workshop. Life, his family, his friends and experience were his workshop. And what a glorious workshop it was, and the most valuable lesson in appreciation and gratitude I can think of to date.

You see, I'd lived my life in a state of 'what's next?' I was always focusing on the future and succumbing to my anxieties about it and how I was seen in the world, as well as holding others to the idea I had adopted (from where I don't know) of how they or things were supposed to be. I was literally terrified. Terrified to jump in the pool because my body wasn't perfect, terrified to be around people that were different than me – whether perceived 'higher' or 'lower' than me. Something I know now to be an illusionary product of societal conditioning, but all along there it was. My brother and his living, breathing example of the way he lived – his bounce-back 'don't give a fuck' perception – had once scared but now inspires me. I truly wish that it didn't take his death for me to learn such a valuable lesson.

My previous experiences, however, had not given me the magnitude of suffering and pain that this experience has. From the deep emotional rollercoaster to the physical symptoms that had me feeling as if I wasn't long for this world either, to witnessing the unbearable suffering my mother, his wife and three children endured.

You might ask how I could ever cultivate gratitude from the experience. How does anyone who's had to endure such deep suffering find it within them? Some days it took everything in me to even stand up. I remember a conversation I had with my mother where she cried out, saying she didn't even have the strength to move, and my words to her were, 'Just stand up, take the first step, and then the second, and by some force, you will be given the strength to take the next.' I don't know where this strength comes from, but it's real. However, you have to meet it half way.

My brother and grandmother both believe this strength comes from Jesus. That like the Footprints poem that once sat on my night table, when we're in our deepest tragedies, we are by some mystical force carried through. My personal belief is that this force is innate from birth. And that throughout our lives it's constantly whispering to us and we, as I've said over and over again, just need to be still enough to hear it. That voice is our most radical authentic self. And whatever medium we use to get there is our own personal choice. And though perhaps we don't see things in the same way, much like my brother and I, I respect whatever it is for you.

'Thank you, Jesus,' is something I had been used to hearing my entire life, as I grew up, like most Anglos, close to the Christian faith. And as life would have it, 'thank you' through prayer with my grandmother, would be my brother's last words before his passing. As I recall from my conversation with my grandmother, their very last conversation was filled with questions for Heaven and his final prayer was how he was thankful for every experience and connection that he had been blessed with. What a last conversation and prayer to have. The kind you most often read about in books or see in movies. But this is real. And the catalyst to a powerful shift, and perspective on gratitude for me.

Up until this conversation I had longed to feel what it felt like to be grateful no matter what, but I struggled with defiant replies as I saw the gratitude quotes go by on my social media. How can you be grateful for such tragedies? In my experience there is no easy way. **The only way to healing, to a greater understanding and to higher wisdom, is through the pain.** Not to take the path already beaten to a pulp but the one we must beat ourselves. It takes courage, strength and tenacity – or what they call blood, sweat and tears. But believe me, it's the only way. Experience, and being totally present to what we are feeling and fully processing, that is the only way. And once we're there, we will be able to look back with the light of a deeper awareness.

***

And it took this tragedy for me to fully experience and embody gratitude in and for everything. After all, the worst of the worst happened, and here I and my entire family were, with a choice to either be consumed by darkness or let his life, his message, be the light of awareness that carries us through.

And for me, even though I still wake up many days crying, wishing and hoping he would come walking through that door, I remember the light he brought to our lives. I remember the gratitude he had for everything, his last prayer, and the ripple effect it all had in my own awareness of gratitude.

And every time I feel myself slipping into a state of ungratefulness, I close my eyes and I see his smile, his amazing smile, forever etched on my heart, reminding me of the power of gratitude to shape our experiences, no matter where life has and will take us. And every day, as his last prayer, I cultivate the light of awareness within to be grateful for all things. Because all things have contributed to who I am today.

The Practice of Gratitude

Appreciation for What/Who's Good

It's challenging when we're in the midst of chaos and suffering but essential too, as Cher said in *Moonstruck* (I'm aging myself again): 'Snap out of it!' Not that we need to snap out of or bypass what we're feeling, because that's very real and a very necessary part of the process, but we must allow the light of awareness to penetrate our perception.

When 'the going gets tough', it can send us on a downward spiral. We get on the negative train to Darkville that can sometimes be overwhelming to return from. But if we take a moment, perhaps between tears, to cultivate gratitude for the good things, experiences and people that we are blessed with, it can make or break us.

I've not always been able to 'practice what I preach', but when I do, this practice has been a life saver. Both when I returned from an unconscious state after trying to take my own life as a teen, and in the months following my brother's sudden death. Yes, the experiences that surrounded me were grim; however, there was also so much in reality to be grateful for. As a teen the rush of support from family and close friends which was literally lifesaving, to know that you are seen and loved could make the difference that led to the experiences I am writing about today. And in the passing of my brother not just the people that 'showed up', but how deeply they showed up filled my soul with a level of gratitude that seriously felt like I was high, naturally, without the influence of substance. And to hear the stories of how he touched people's lives, to know how he touched his children's, his wife's and my own life gave me butterflies that carried me through even the darkest of times. It gave me the light I needed to step in the right direction.

The circumstances don't have to be as tragic. There are opportunities in every experience every day that can provide us with a greater understanding of gratitude, and create the catalyst to lift us higher or maybe just carry us through.

Take a moment now to appreciate what's good. Perhaps they are small things, but just like taking baby steps eventually leads to running, building on the little things leads to a greater perspective that can save a life, or even just a day.

Remembering What's Made You

You're a beautiful person inside and out. Yes you are. I know perhaps you've thought, said or done things that are 'out of character' but at the core you are a beautiful radiant being. I know this to be true. And it's through life experiences that we have the opportunity to cultivate the awareness.

Remember what's made you – the light and the dark. Life is both yin and yang and hopefully we come to a place where as the pendulum swings we don't allow it to define us but use the contrast to remember who we are.

The light has shaped us; however, from my own experience the darkness has the ability to shape us even more. The darkest experiences in my life have led me to the deepest perspectives, and once through them they have lit the path to the awareness that has brought me to where I am today.

Being abused as a child both sexually and physically, with a lot of psychological, physical, and spiritual work, has moulded me and made me the man I am today. Would I ask for it all again? The jury is out on that one. Don't judge me or think that I want it to happen to anyone else, or that I condone such behaviour, but it awakened in me a place of deep non-biased compassion for people, both the victims and perpetrators. Not that one shouldn't be held accountable for one's actions – the projection of our pain in whatever form is never acceptable. However, once I was able to see my abusers as humans, disconnected and in deep pain, I was able to forgive and to free myself from the experience. It has been a lifetime's work.

I'm not asking, or even expecting, that you do, or even can do the same. But what I am asking is that you perhaps take a journey through your life, if you're capable, and work to find gratitude for the experiences both light and dark, and reframe them in a manner that makes you feel a little lighter in the loafers. Do please see a professional for guidance if this is needed. Life, even in its simplest day, can be challenging and the more we're able to reframe our experiences with gratitude for how they've shaped our lives, the easier we sleep. And there's nothing better than a good night's sleep.

Gratitude Reflection (Meditation)
Taking a journey down memory lane can provide us with an instant dose of joy. Perhaps this isn't the right practice with which to visit the dark experiences. Let's just use this practice to focus on the light, and what's lifted you higher.

Take a few minutes in the morning, during a break or in the evening – whatever works best for you – and close your eyes and take yourself through the experiences that have brought you the most joy. Start with maybe one experience from today, or if you can't find one, then bring in a recent experience.

Focus on the experience as if you were taking a tour with the Ghost of Christmas Past (*A Christmas Carol*). Relive it through your mind and allow yourself all the feelings. Every time I utilize this practice I get goosepimples which are always a sign for me that it's an experience I enjoy and the feeling of joy is, for me, a precursor to gratitude. Just like when someone gifted me with food as a kid, first the joy, then the gratitude.

My mind can be like a drunken monkey and so this practice can take a lot of practice. Some days it's a breeze and some days our memories are covered in clouds, but as the great Maya Angelou said: 'there's always a rainbow in the clouds'. Just keep looking. You'll find it, and then ride it like a dream. Allow it to penetrate you with joy and cultivate a deep vibrating sense of gratitude. And the more you practice, the better you get. **Practice is the key to transforming our patterns from self-defeating to self-improving.**

Act with Love

Ah, love. Sweet love. What the world needs now is more love. Such truth, and so many obstacles to truth and love. Layers upon layers of conditioning and resistance can make it really challenging to access the love. And to act from that place, as best we can, in all things.

But like all things, we start with the little things. We start where we are and when we can we expand from there. Maybe it's just loving your morning coffee or sitting on your porch (or someone else's if you don't have one) and appreciating the effortlessness of nature; how as Lao Tzu said, it 'does not hurry yet everything is accomplished'. Or watching the plethora of cat videos that go by on your Facebook feed.

I could be doing the dishes. I'm using this example because I hate doing dishes, but it's a great reference for me because I've used it from time to time to practice this principle. When I'm completely present and loving the process, it makes a huge difference. I 'crank the tunes' (a phrase I learned from my mother early in life as she passed along her love of music) and smell the dish soap (I love to smell everything, a weird habit of mine). I fill the sink with warm water, and I giver (a term I learned in the ghetto) and while I'm in the process, dancing away, the feeling of loving what I'm doing and being completely present begins to help me cultivate a state of awareness for what I have to be grateful.

In order for there to be dishes I have to have eaten something, and in order to have eaten something I had to have the means to shop for it, and there creates the ripple effect of gratitude that has me appreciating everything from the delicious meal I ate, to the means to eat it, to gratitude for my health, and the gift of being able to see, feel, and hear everything in the process. Whatever act, however little, start there. Infuse love into your action(s) and take it from there.

And the gratitude just keeps expanding ... I'm grateful for the home that houses the dishes, for the experiences that led to the sink being full, to my mom for teaching me to wash them, when I hated it and thought she was the devil for making me do them. Now I appreciate the lesson which I didn't get then. As well as the time I got to spend with her doing them.

So give it a try. Take something little. Water the plants (if you have them), or take the dog for a walk, or give the dishwasher a break and wash them by hand. But use the process to cultivate loving kindness, and a sense of appreciation for all that it is. And watch your sense of gratitude grow in leaps and bounds. Far greater than you might expect from something so simple. It's in the little things.

Reflection: Find a Good Place to Start

When you're in the moment, and if the experience has caused or causes you deep suffering it's difficult to experience gratitude for it or for anything. You may just want to punch whoever in the face (don't do it) even if you've processed matters enough to access that emotion. Perhaps you're too deep in depression or anxiety to even access such a basic emotion as anger. And from my experience you need to sit there with that, with the heaviness and the feelings and allow it all to move through you, without keeping you stuck in it.

You need to keep moving and experiencing things until they pass, before you can cultivate the gratitude for the experience to take you higher.

And you get to decide when that is for you, when you're ready. And until the pain of remaining the same is worse than the fear you have of facing it, you'll stay there. And you may never move from that space. Perhaps you don't have it in you. Perhaps life has given you so many lemons you don't have the strength to make lemonade, and to sit on the porch enjoying it. However, I believe, if you're reading this book, you have it within you. You may need a little inspiration, motivation or professional assistance. But you've got it, the light is there. Start with baby steps. Start right now and be grateful that you had the strength to find this book.

It's a good place to start your appreciation practice. Today.

CHAPTER 11
GOTTA MOVE, GOTTA GET OUT – MOVEMENT

Gotta move, gotta get out!

This I know for sure. Our movement, whether through moving our bodies or taking a step in the direction of our desires, is most definitely key to our wellbeing and fulfillment. **We have to participate relentlessly in the manifestation of our desires – taking action, and creating movement physically, mentally and spiritually.**

Moving our body through walking, yoga, or jogging (whatever body movement that you truly desire and enjoy, not the latest trend just because everyone else is doing it) is as crucial as taking action mentally and spiritually through personal development and stepping in the direction of our desires, taking risks and having the tenacity to follow through. You just have to keep moving, or as Dory said in *Finding Nemo* 'just keep swimming, just keep swimming'. Just don't sit there and think about it, get up and act even if it's just baby steps. Movement is crucial to our mental, physical and spiritual health.

Scientists have stated that sitting still is the new cancer, that it begins to destroy our bodies from the inside out. It slowly deteriorates our body and eventually has a grave impact on our mental and spiritual wellbeing as well. **We are not meant to be static beings. We're designed to be on the move, searching, gathering, connecting; nourishing our mind, body and soul**

along the way. But somewhere along the line we've become disconnected from our natural rhythm and have become an industrialized society that majorly spends our time sitting, typing, scrolling and, when we perhaps think of getting up to move, we are overwhelmed by the plethora of information being thrown at us, and it can get really exhausting.

What do we choose? Which modality? Yoga? Tai Chi? Cross Fit? Weight training?

Yesterday that one was the best, today this one, and tomorrow another. It can be so hard to catch up with what experts are saying is the best movement. And I'm not just talking about exercise, I'm talking about the movement that's required to fulfill our desires. Every morning when I pick up my phone (a habit I am trying to kick) there is article after article pulling me in every which direction. No – this way to your desires – no, this way. Everyone has the key, and then when that key is debunked someone will come up with another, and another, and so we get wrapped up in following the crowd, most of the time, if not every time, disconnected from our own natural rhythm. And our devices are increasingly being designed to keep us that way. They want us engaged with the collective, the ultimate consuming machine. **But what's most important isn't what anybody else has to say, or any expert or trend is claiming as 'the best' or 'the way'; what's most important is that 'the best' or 'the way' is your best or your way.** That is if you even have the mental capacity to figure it out in the first place.

Many of us live static lives out of a lack of motivation. Or perhaps a lack of options. Maybe we've fallen into a deep depression, which can be quite easy to do in our current climate. Or we have limited options as what we do to 'make ends meet' keeps us trapped in a desk behind a computer for hours each day or requires hours upon hours of attention to social media and what the rest of the world is doing – what the media and marketeers want us to focus on. But, whatever the case, it is of utmost importance that we make it our top priority to keep moving.

I remember one of my teachers saying to me, 'When you stop moving, you die.' It kind of scared the shit out of me because at that time I took it quite literally, and have grown to discover that it is quite literal. Not only does our body begin to die, but so does our motivation and inspiration, which carries our drive to grow, walk in the direction of our desires, and achieve our own personal fulfillment.

Lack of movement can create a downward spiral in our lives that holds us hostage from ourselves and truly living a radically authentic, fulfilled life. 'But I truly am lazy,' you might say. 'I love just vegging out on the couch binge watching Netflix,' 'I don't have any energy when I get home from work,' or 'I lack the will to move because I've been inundated with more than I can handle' and 'I'm just exhausted.' And I get it, believe me. I get that, I've been there, many times in my life, too many to count actually. Lack of movement has been my go-to when times get tough, when life knocks me down, and it's a bitch to get back up. And it can lead to deeper depression, addiction, and a downward spiral that never ends, in some cases costing us our life.

But we have to move, if we truly desire to live our best lives. We've got be able to 'fall down seven times and get up eight' which has become somewhat of my motto. It doesn't mean you can't rest a while, give your body, mind and spirit a rest. Take a day off, a retreat, or even just a few hours. All of those things are crucial for rejuvenation and healing. However, we must get up, dust ourselves off, and try it again.

Start with a 15-minute walk, then maybe kick it up to a speed-walk, a bike ride if you own one, or put on your favourite tune and dance your ass off (a personal fave). Whatever it is, we've got to just keep moving, keeping our minds, bodies and spirits active and engaged. The more active we are the more vibrant we feel and the higher our vibe the deeper our connection to the truth of ourselves. And being active and engaged is about more than physical activity and health. It's also about getting out and connecting with people,

people that are in alignment with who we truly are and where we want to be. They say we become the five people we spend the most time with, so look around, take inventory. Is that who you are, or what you want to become?

Also we must become proactive participants in the manifestation of our desires. We take ten steps towards our desires and magically our desires move closer. But this requires action and relentless participating and continuing to check in with ourselves to make sure that we're on our track, not somebody else's.

It really is quite magical when we're walking our path with intention and how we discover the interrelation of movement with our mind, body and spirit. When we feel low, depressed or stuck in life, just taking a short walk in nature, participating in a game of tennis, kicking a ball around or doing Yoga can be the catalyst we need to shake the negative energy from our bodies, clear our minds and catapult us in the direction of our deepest truth. **Our bodies are not unlike the universe, self-organizing and self-healing, but not without our participation.**

My Story: Moving Through Grief

I've been rather static for the last week after the spreading of my brother's ashes. To watch his children and wife pour his ashes in the water at his favourite fishing spot just tore me apart, rehashed a lot of emotions, and has had me static ever since. Like a deer in headlights. I have no motivation, no inspiration. I just wanted to sit here being sad, doing nothing.

Tragic circumstances can knock us down and out, sometimes taking days, weeks and even months to gain enough energy to even do the smallest of tasks. And there is no time limit on grief, whatever it is you're grieving – whether it's the loss of a job, separation from your spouse, a friendship gone south, or, in my case, the sudden loss of a sibling.

However, as life would have it, we most often don't have the time to grieve as long as we perhaps would allow ourselves to, as the world is calling us back, and remaining static, as we know, not only affects our physical health, but our mental, spiritual and, yes, even our financial wellbeing. The longer we stay static without movement or action the worse it all gets. I know this to be true.

After my brother passed away, at first I felt a force of energy overtake my body so intensely that I felt like a warrior, and then the further away from the events surrounding his death the lower became my energy, my drive, and my motivation to move. I would just lie on the couch for days weeping, asking over and over again, why? And there were no answers.

This wasn't like the self-inquiry I was used to that provided me with the feedback I'd use to understand myself, because the answers came up empty. There was no reason. And so this sent me on a rollercoaster of confusion, of trying to grasp, to hold onto something. All the while I was mustering up what strength I could to be the light for my mother, father and my brother's family.

I went deeper and deeper into a static state, the most movement I can remember was moving from my bed to the couch. I didn't even have the strength to eat or shower. But the world was still moving and going on around me. Nothing or no one stopped or was going to. No matter what my state, life was still happening around me. I just couldn't feel it. But these feelings I was having, this lack of motivation and inspiration, weren't new, but they had been intensified by what I had experienced. So intense that my blood pressure had risen to dangerous levels, making me afraid for my own life. Previously this lack of motivation that manifested as a lack of desire to move had been less intense, and shorter, and I was able to rest for a short while and get back up. But this time, it required every ounce of strength I had left.

I've often coined my superpower as resilience, and so even though I lacked the energy to get up I knew that it was there for me to access. I built on whatever light I could feel day after day until I finally gained the strength to stand, and then to walk, and then to shower, and then, well, I headed right to the fridge (I covered this in Chapter 7: 'What We Put In, We Get Out'). And once I gained the motivation to start moving. I googled 'Yoga postures for grief', as I knew that Yoga through physical movement and mental decluttering was a saviour. At least in my experience.

At this point I was in jeopardy of losing everything. I had stopped writing, engaging, and all production on a product line I was testing with my husband. I was desperately reaching out to my husband continuously, to the point where he was in great fear of my physical and mental health, taking him away from his own means of financial survival. Our finances began to take a massive dip and I knew I had to muster up whatever strength I had within, as after suffering the major loss of my brother I wasn't ready to lose myself.

So I took action, in baby steps of course. I started with Yoga for grief as the first thing I did when I woke up, and as I began to feel the almost magical healing effect of Yoga, I introduced a five-minute Meditation practice (baby steps) Day by day I mustered up the strength to get up (fall down seven times, get up eight) and practice. After a few weeks I began to feel alive again. I started to write, to engage and to pick up where I had left off the day I received the call that would change my life and perspective forever.

And as I practiced the movements that worked for me, everything about me started to feel better, vibrant, more alive, motivated and inspired. So, as I could, I incorporated more and more movement into my daily routine. I was starting the day with Yoga, Meditation and then adding a walk in nature, and every day in every way the pain began to fall away and the wisdom from self-inquiry began to fill me with the inspiration I needed to keep reaching higher and higher.

I began to hear that song playing over and over in my head again, 'This little light of mine, I'm gonna let it shine, this little light of mine, I'm gonna let it shine, let it shine, let it shine, let it shine.' And there I was again, captain of my ship, steering towards the light. And the more I moved, the more motivation I had to move and the healthier I felt in my mind, body and spirit. I was really captivated by how much of an impact moving my physical body had on my wellbeing. I mean, I worked in the gym industry for a number of years and I was certain of the effect it had on our/my physical health, but never had I experienced the vastness of its ability to clear the mind.

Metaphysically I had heard (probably in one of the many workshops I attended) that we hold our emotional pain in our physical bodies and that movement is key to our healing and fulfillment; however, I had never experienced it first-hand, and as powerfully as I had through this experience.

***

Most of my life I've fought with motivation physically. Perhaps it was due to what I had been carrying in my body physically. It was literally weighing me down. I gained the perspective to understand everything is in relation to and affects the other; our mind speaks our body, our body speaks our mind. Incorporating mindful movement in my life, the kind of movement that I enjoyed, brought me the lightness in body and clarity of mind that walks me home to my most radically authentic self. And so now when I wake up lazy, feeling worn down by the weight of the world, I am reminded of the power of movement to make me feel good in my body, to clear negative energy, to shift my perspective and lead me towards the light of my own awareness.

The Practice of Movement

Walk
'Walk it off' is a phrase I remember hearing a lot as a kid, and again as an adult by my dear friend Diana. It was her father's philosophy. It's a lot of people's really. From as far back as I can remember I have memories of walking with my mom and

grandmother. We would walk everywhere. And I remember the feeling of both exhaustion and fulfillment when we were done. Not only did my body feel relieved, but my mind eased of whatever was stressing me. Walking together with your mom, friend or partner is also great therapy, it gets the juices flowing. Whenever I am feeling a lack of inspiration or just in a foul mood, I walk.

Walking has been praised for its amazing physical health benefits and ability to improve the quality and physical length of our life, and it is now being extensively studied for its ability to reduce stress; induce serotonin (happy hormones); improve clarity, self-confidence and cognitive ability; boost brain activity; sharpen our memory; increase relaxation, spark our creative genius; help with addiction and inspire others. Wow, the list just goes on and on.

For me specifically, walking helps me clear negative energy, mind chatter, and channel my creative genius. And YES, it helps me with my addiction to food. Usually when I'm about to emotionally binge eat it is a psychological trigger, and so to take a brisk walk in nature helps to clear and get clear on whatever's coming up for me.

It's also a great tool to save relationships! It's where my theology of conscious action (peace) versus reaction (war) comes in. Most often when we're triggered, especially when we're physically and mentally exhausted, we tend to react, which can create a neverending conflict, like a ping-pong match. However, if we practice conscious action and literally walk away, or take a hike, every single time (at least in my experience) we come back with a clearer understanding of what happened and what we actually wanted to communicate.

Walking seems to me the miracle cure. It can help us with a plethora of physical and mental challenges but its key benefit is how it contributes to our clarity of focus and the higher awareness of our most authentic selves.

Breathe

Ahhhhh! 'Close your eyes, relax your body, and take a deep breath in through your nose and into your belly. Open your mouth, and release.' If you've ever taken a Yoga class this sequence will be very familiar. As will the feeling you have after you practice. Pranayama is what it's referred to in Yoga philosophy, Prana meaning 'life force' in Sanskrit. **Our breath literally is our life force and the mindful control of it can make or break us when it comes to managing our wellbeing.**

The first time I heard of using the breath as a tool was when I was in the hospital going through intensive therapy after trying to take my own life. The practitioner I was working with handed me a paper bag and told me to take the bag, put it up to my mouth and focus on breathing out and in when my anxiety started to heighten. It was a life saver. As my anxiety would rise I would use the paper bag trick as a practice, and sometimes within seconds I would be calm. Bringing myself to a state of clarity and awareness where I could access the truth of the moment versus the rambling stories in my monkey mind that led to the attack.

As I began to grow, so did my practices. As part of my Yoga teacher training, I learned the deeper practice of using breathwork to manage our daily lives. When we connect with the breath we are tuned into the present moment and in the present moment we have access to the truth of ourselves.

Breathwork as a practice has a plethora of benefits to both our mind and body. It releases toxins from our body, relieves pain and tension, boosts the immune system, helps us process and release our emotions, elevates our mood and our awareness, and vastly increases our energy, so making us more resilient and capable of moving through stressors with ease.

'Breathing in, I calm body and mind. Breathing out, I smile. Dwelling in the present moment, I know this is the only moment.'

Thich Nhat Hanh

One of my absolute favourite breathing techniques that I learned in Yoga teacher training is called *Durga Pranyama* or Three Part Breath. It's my go-to when the going gets tough, when I've become distracted and disconnected, and when I want to get in touch with my inner self to guide me in making the decisions with my truest self.

Give it a try now if you'd like, and if you like to use mantras (a word or sound repeated to aid concentration) this is one of my favourites. It gives me the goosepimples every time I say it.

1. Now get seated comfortably, or lie down if that works better for you.
2. Close your eyes, relax your tongue from the roof of your mouth and connect to the natural rhythm of your breath. Stay there for a few moments noticing what you notice.
3. Then, you take a deep breath into your belly and say 'Breathing in, I calm my body and mind.'
4. And as you breathe out: 'Breathing out I smile.' And smile, a big one like Ketut in *Eat Pray Love* – 'Smile with your liver.'
5. Once relaxed into your natural rhythm take a deep breath in through your nose, deep into your belly, and then out through your nose again. With the next breath, on the inhale bring the breath into your belly again and then up into the bottom of your ribcage so you feel your ribs expand and release. Breathe out through your nose of course, and lastly take another deep breath in through your nose, into your belly, up into your ribcage and finally expanding around your heart, and release.
6. Repeat this for as little or as long as you want. I guarantee that whatever you are struggling with, this technique will give you a space of peace, and clarity.

Our breath is our life force, it can both sustain and take our life away. So to be conscious of it, and to use it as a force to connect to our highest self and operate from that space, is key to an authentic, fulfilled life.

Mindful Movement

Whether it's Yoga, Tai Chi, Karate or dance, mindful movement is a catalyst to releasing resistance and connecting to the truth of who we are. However, not all Yoga classes use mindful movement. I've been to many a Yoga class that felt completely mindless, with the focus being on the end result versus a deep connection in presence to our physical, mental and spiritual bodies.

Mindful movement always reminds me of a Wayne Dyer quote, one that I heard him speak about regularly: 'When you dance, your purpose is not to get to a certain place on the floor. It's to enjoy each step along the way.' And such is the purpose of mindful movement. To be deeply present, connected and moving with intention. *Intention* being the key word.

The majority of our physical and mental movements, unless we practice and operate from a state of awareness, are mindless and disconnected. In class perhaps we're paying more attention to our neighbours' bodies than our own, or alone we're distracted by the clock and just getting it done. And our distracted conscious keeps us separate from what's going on in our bodies, our minds and from hearing the whispers of our soul.

'The quieter we become the more we can hear' is a Ram Dass quote I use often, both as a reminder for myself and a reminder for you. It's the ultimate truth; when we're quiet we can hear what our bodies, minds or spirits are trying to communicate. And mindful movement is a fast track (that's not so fast) to that place. We don't need to worry about what to do next, or what's the next Yoga posture, but just hanging out there in Downward Dog feeling every sensation, hearing every thought, taking a breath and allowing ourselves to go deeper. Many times I've been in Yoga class in such a deep sense of presence, and fully submerged in a posture only to come to and realize the class is over and it's time for Savasana (a restorative posture usually practiced at the end of a class). And that's ok, because the purpose of mindful movement is to be mindful and present, paying attention to ourselves and then operating from that space of authenticity in everything we do.

Another mindful movement I really enjoy is dancing, although sometimes if I've had a few glasses it might not be all that mindful, or is it? I mean – after a few glasses of gin I most often feel a deep sense of relaxation and presence. So perhaps I become a more mindful dancer as I'm not worried what every else is thinking of my moves. Which by the way are pretty bloody fantastic!

But whatever mindful movement gets you into that space, where there's nothing but presence – just you, and your truest self – do your best to work that into your daily routine. It's not only a great way to move your body but it's playful as well, at least it is for me. Which reminds me of the time I let one loose in Yoga class only to be shamed, but we'll leave that story for another time. Or you can ask me about it when you see me around …

Reflection: One Foot in Front of the Other
So we've gotta move. This I know for sure.

We've got to keep active and engaged in a mindful way. Whether it's through physical movement of our body, breathwork, or stepping out of our static lives and jumping into something exciting, something that helps us grow, perhaps a journey to another country or maybe even just up the road. Road trips are a great way to get a move on, perhaps to experience new things, meet new people and who knows, maybe you'll even find a new class (this is where the letting loose in a Yoga class story comes in)? Or perhaps you travel to a new world, which can open you up to yourself in so many different ways. You're always welcome to join us on one of our VividLife Journeys, the info is on my website at VividLife.me.

As a child I had no idea I would travel the world to Japan, Africa, Ireland, India and beyond. I gotta move on it, I relentlessly participated in the manifestation of my desires and I put one foot in front of the other, taking baby steps until I looked back from the other side of the world. I learned so much about myself. I learned new ideas and modalities for mindful movement. I got inspired to take action, and I inspired others to join me, to take a stand against their static lives, lives that had them (and me) on repeat slowly dying to ourselves, to the truth of who we were and conforming to the collective.

Our movement is key. If we stay still we not only cease to grow but we eventually die, not only to the truth of who we are, but eventually to our bodies. So get up, stand up, take a baby step, or perhaps a leap and be relentless in the quest for your radically authentic life.

CHAPTER 12

NOTHING YOU BECOME WILL DISAPPOINT ME – UNCONDITIONAL LOVE AND COMPASSION

'Nothing you become will disappoint me.' Let that be your mantra. Let that be all of our mantras. Let unconditional love be the very foundation of our intentions, of ourself and of others. It doesn't mean we don't hold ourselves and others accountable, but what it does mean is that we love in spite of.

Wikipedia describes unconditional love as 'love without conditions'. Love without conditions. Imagine that. Imagine a love like that. One where you wake up every morning no matter where you are in life, no matter what the conditions and you just love yourself, right where you're at, in all your glory or messiness. Imagine that you forgive yourself for making 'mistakes', for not making the honour roll in high school, for skipping college to travel the world, for claiming bankruptcy, lashing out when you were hurt, or having a few lazy days when life knocked you down.

Because, aside from those experiences, you are a radiantly authentic being, born with the limitless potential to be yourself. Whatever that looks like. Whether you're a doctor, a lawyer, a musician, artist or a laborer, whether you live in a big mansion in Hollywood or a tiny house on Vancouver Island, if that's who you truly are then own that, and love yourself in that space unconditionally. Let go of the idea that everything and everyone, including yourself, needs to look, act, and reach a certain goal or status to be loved. You are worthy of that love right this moment. You are the champion, the one sperm that made it to the egg, creating and birthing a magnificent human being.

'It doesn't matter what your mama did. It doesn't matter what your daddy didn't do. You are responsible for your life.'
Oprah Winfrey

And you are responsible for the amount of love you let in and give out, and for undoing the conditions that hold you hostage to it. We have been conditioned our whole life that we must 'do' in order to be valued or loved. And that's bullshit. Who decides? Where is this list of what makes us worthy or not worthy of love? And who is the one keeping score, *except* ourselves? After all, everything begins and ends with ourselves. We wake up and go to bed with ourselves and so ultimately we are the ones who choose.

And as Rupaul says, 'If you don't love yourself, how in the hell you gonna love somebody else?' Especially with a list full of conditions – conditions which all become barriers to living our lives in radical, authentic love. When we limit love, we limit life. When everything and everyone must show up in a certain way. When our definition of love both of self and others is limited to conditions, we miss out on the depth of emotional vulnerability and spiritual growth that leads us to a profound understanding of who we are; stardust, the cosmic hands of the universe exploring itself. We perceive everything through our conditioning which is based on a collective of what we've experienced and what we've been told. Our beliefs. And often times our beliefs limit instead of expand us. Getting stuck in our beliefs is often the nemesis of unconditional love of self and others. Let's take for instance that in your family there's an expectation that you go to college, get a corporate career, get married, have kids, buy a house and start saving for retirement and so you happen to not meet that expectation. You're an artist with a gypsy soul who doesn't want kids and loves to travel the world never really staying too long in one place. And the push back for you to be what's considered 'normal' creates a belief that for some reason you're less than, and not worthy of love, maybe it was something that was spoken, or perhaps it was an uncomfortable silence, either way it became an obstruction to your unbiased love of yourself because you didn't meet the conditions required.

Politics is another example, an extremely amplified one. Everyone must believe what you believe in order to be accepted. You could say that politics, religion and any group based on an ideology or system of beliefs is the cause for this separation, or amplification of a collection of expectations and beliefs that must be adhered to in order to be accepted (loved). But behind each of these groups, the commonality is people. Individuals who at any time have the free will to believe what they want to believe, and love who they want to love, including themselves, unconditionally.

Yes. You are that. We are all it. And the sooner we understand that the better off we will be, both individually and collectively. **Any love we withhold from ourselves we're withholding from the whole, and what the world needs now more than ever is love.** We need the kind of unconditional love that heals, that magically inspires us to follow our highest good, to throw ourselves a buoy when we've perhaps been treading water too long. We need the love that brings food to the homeless, that wraps a criminal in arms of love because we love ourselves so much that our love unconditionally overflows to others. Without conditions. Sure, it's easier to love ourselves when we've got the accolades and the money, or it's easier to love a sick child, or a family that's experienced a natural disaster than it is to love a criminal. But do we really love if that love is conditional? Again, I'm not saying that people must not be held accountable for their actions, including ourselves. But what I am saying may sound radical to you, and it is, because it requires us to dig into the depths of our radically authentic selves to find the place that lives in us all, that recognizes that we are one. It recognises that we need each other, and that it's our responsibility when blessed with the gift of that awareness to bestow that on others.

I recently read of a tribe in Africa that when someone does something that perhaps we might deem as hurtful, or criminal, the entire tribe gets together, forms a circle and surrounds them for two days reminding them of everything good they have ever done, of who they are aside from whatever affliction or disconnected state that brought them to do what they've done. Because this tribe believes, as I do (which may be utopian but it's my belief and I get to hold onto it), that every human being comes into this world as good, that each of us desires security, peace, happiness and love. And that this act of disconnection is a cry for acknowledgement or love. A cry for help. And so as a community, they stand together to remind them and reconnect them of their true nature, of their true self.

Fact or fiction, this brings tears to my eyes, both as an example of the kind of love that really heals humanity and of a powerful example of how we can use this theology not only with others, but with ourselves, so that when we become disconnected from the truth of who we are, we love ourselves back to life, unconditionally.

Love, of self, and others, is contagious. **And our unconditional love of ourselves is not only the catalyst of liberation, but the foundation upon which we can build a life in deep alignment with who we are.** When there are conditions on love, there's resistance to it, and the more resistance to love, the deeper our suffering. Let it be your mission, beginning with yourself, to bring your awareness to all the obstacles you have to love, and one by one remove them, invoking a sense of radical authenticity one only sees in the likes of Nobel laureates and saints. Who, I might add, were all born of the same stardust as you. They just choose to nurture the goodness within, and to love themselves and others, unconditionally.

My Story: Listen Up, the Dalai Lama's Speaking

Before that day, love and compassion to me were something I had for others. Most directly for people that were very close to me, and the suffering of children, animals or innocent people. However, that love and compassion didn't include myself or those who I felt didn't deserve it. Consistently beating myself up for making what I once considered mistakes, and holding others accountable to my conditioned understanding of what deserved love and compassion, I gave love and compassion in relation to what and who I felt deserved it. And when I heard that the Dalai Lama was coming to a city close to me to do a talk on unbiased compassion I immediately logged on to buy tickets for my husband and me, as I longed to be more at peace with myself and with others.

My husband and I arrived that day to an auditorium of thousands of people, all eager to hear the wisdom of the Dalai Lama. What had sparked my interest in hearing him speak was a book of his that I read on my journey to Tokyo called *The Art of Happiness*, which was one of the few books besides *The Four Agreements* by Don Miguel Ruiz that I had actually read. Which reminds me of what my husband would often say: 'reading is for prisoners'. And, well, I once felt that way too, until I fell upon literature that would become the catalyst to waking me up. And *The Art of Happiness* is to be included, and just so happens to include one of the most poignant messages I can remember to date: 'Love and compassion are necessities, not luxuries. Without them, humanity cannot survive.' And this I know to be true, today.

However, at that time in my life, not only had I just begun the journey to undoing conditioning and learning to be aware of the resistance that came with it, but I was still carrying an immense amount of pain, unresolved emotions and anger, which would get projected unconsciously in many situations and on many people who perhaps didn't deserve it but had accidently triggered the pain. And for years I regretted my actions and the relationships that suffered that expense.

And this talk on unbiased compassion felt like the key to redemption's door. Both for the love and compassion I held from myself, and the love and compassion I held from others who had hurt me both consciously and unconsciously. I was withholding a whole lot of love, especially from myself, around whom I built a suit of armour to protect myself from any further suffering. But what I know now, that I didn't know then, is that it's impossible to avoid, that the world just keeps handing it to us in whatever form and that the more compassion and love we give to ourselves and others, the easier it is to get through. Because, as the Dalai Lama had said, it's our very nature, and when we're connected to our true nature, we connect to ourselves.

'I believe all suffering is caused by ignorance. People inflict pain on others in the selfish pursuit of their happiness or satisfaction. Yet true happiness comes from a sense of inner peace and contentment, which in turn must be achieved through the cultivation of altruism, of love and compassion and elimination of ignorance, selfishness and greed.'

Dalai Lama

And from that day on my practice in non-biased compassion, which I see as the precursor to love, became my core mission. I looked back through my life and began to see the others who had harmed me through physical, mental, and sexual abuse and bullying – to see them in the tribal circle of remembrance and to remind myself who they were at their core, how they had been disconnected for whatever reason, and how their actions towards me were not a reflection of my worth and ability to be loved, but a reflection of their own pain and selfish pursuit at the cost of mine. Through this practice I began to look at all my experiences, both with others and alone, and began to see them with a heart of compassion.I did this in order to eliminate all the obstacles I had built to loving myself and others without conditions.

***

I flipped through my life like a storybook, stopping at each section where I felt pain and using my new-found wisdom to reflect on and release it. The experience took many, many years, and came in many difficult layers, and the more difficult the longer I sat with it. There were so many painful experiences and people that felt unforgivable that it took every ounce of spiritual light I could find to see in the eyes of love and compassion, including myself.

But I worked at it, and worked at it – baby steps every day, in every way I could. Some days it was more difficult than others, but the more I was able to see it all with the wisdom of non-biased love and compassion the freer I became, and the more liberated in authenticity my actions. I felt fewer lash-outs, less self-harm. It seemed that the armour that I had built up to protect myself was crashing to the ground, the heaviness turned to lightness, the pressure released and my world began to look like a vivid painting filled with light, radiant hearts and the possibility of healing and wholeness on the horizon. Everything about myself was transforming; I was a chrysalis of spiritual proportions I'd only dreamed about.

It only took one perspective, in this case through the words of one of the most admired and spiritual people in the world. But without the experiences that brought me to the auditorium that day, I would never have had the shift of awareness that opened the floodgates to the wisdom that walked me home to the truth of who I am, who we all are, at our core.

The Practice of Unconditional Love and Compassion

The Tribal Circle

Just as the African tribe surrounds those who have become disconnected from their truth with a tribal circle of love and remembrance, so should we shower ourselves and others with an abundance of unconditional love and compassion. No matter what we've done, everyone – but firstly ourselves – deserves our unconditional love. And although we may not practice this type of circle in our particular culture – in some cases we have graver consequences for our actions both for our own protection and the protection of others – the idea of the tribal circle is one that I would suggest as a practice to remind ourselves of who we are and what we are deserving of regardless of our actions and afflictions.

Maybe you've had a lazy week, you didn't get the job you interviewed for, you've gained a few pounds, begun to lose your hair, are struggling financially, or struggle with anxiety or anger, and so perhaps when you've done something disconnected, or you haven't lived up to what's been expected of you, just close your eyes and imagine yourself surrounded by a tribal circle of reminders of who you are, what you're capable of, and how regardless of circumstances and outcomes you are worthy of and entitled by birthright to your own unbiased, unconditional love and compassion.

Forgiveness

Ah forgiveness. That word again. If you roll in self-help circles or follow anyone in personal development on social media you have probably read enough on, and seen enough memes reminding you of, the power of forgiveness. The most predominant one that comes to mind is: 'To forgive is to set a prisoner free and discover the prisoner was you.' That is Lewes B. Smedes, and it's true.

Holding onto anything, any energy that creates heaviness in mind, body or spirit, keeps us prisoner to it. And that energy wreaks havoc on our entire system. Some even believe that holding onto the past mistakes and grievances is a precursor to disease (dis-ease) and that our body, our minds and our spirits are not at ease with anything that distracts from our natural state of being, which is peace and harmony.

But how do we forgive? Most importantly, how do we forgive ourselves?

For my entire life forgiveness of others is something that I have been able to achieve. It's like a gift to be able to see through the bullshit straight to the heart. However, it's always been difficult to forgive myself. For most of my life I've carried around feelings of self-condemnation: 'I shouldn't have said that,' 'I shouldn't have done that,' 'I shouldn't have gone there,' and the biggest one: 'I shouldn't have eaten that.' Constantly 'shoulding' on myself. It's quite common really, not just for me but for almost everyone that has ever crossed my path.

We always believe we should have done things differently; however, that perspective comes from the place that we're at, with the wisdom we have today, and looking back on all the things we perhaps could have done differently. We didn't have the experience or knowledge that we do today. And so, if we can come to this understanding we can learn, just like a child that puts his or her hands on a hot surface, that when we know better, we can do better. Then we can begin to work on forgiving ourselves, and releasing ourselves from the self-imposed prison that keeps us hostage from the deeper understanding that no matter which way we choose, if it's our way, it's the right way.

A New Story

'The story' is what we have heard from our beginning and will far outlast us on this earth. Fiction and non-fiction, stories are all around us. Everyone and every living thing has a story but the only creature on the earth that creates them are humans. It's like we constantly have a narrative playing in our head. It's like a 'drunken monkey bit by a scorpion', as the great philosopher Alan Watts once said. Or like the Gremlins running the film in the movie theatre in the 80s cult classic *Gremlins*.

Crazy, erratic, stories of doom and gloom, how we've messed up, how we're going to mess up. The narrative runs amok, sometimes so much so that we develop anxiety, depression and eventually perhaps mental illness. Stories created with bits and pieces from our past merged with ideas we have about how the future will work out. Stories that we must have this, and or do that, that if we do that, or this. That this person is better than us because, or this person is less than, or I have to have this to be this, or if I say this, or don't say that. A war of words battling between our ears distracting us from our own voice – the voice of truth, peace and harmony that loves us unconditionally. And the only way to hear it, as I've said over and over again, is to be still enough to listen. And from that place of silence we can begin to create a new story, one based on fact not on monkey-mind fiction. From the truth of who we are, and from the depths of the creative being of potential we were created to be.

I like to begin creating my new story (or my real story) by reminding myself, usually using the tribal circle, that no matter what I do or become, I am not a disappointment to myself or others because there is nothing to measure against except myself, and myself is something that is consistantly evolving. **The more aware I am of the truth of who I am then the more in harmony I am with the whole.** And then like any creative brainstorming session I highlight my strengths and accomplishments and begin to build a new and empowering story with truth and positivity rather than with a bunch of conditioned bullshit, and fear-based projections that keep me hidden in a prison of disconnection, anxiety and shame. Creating a story that lifts, rather than limits me.

Removing Obstacles

How many obstacles have we created to love both from others and ourselves? How many conditions have we put on when and whether we are worthy of it? It begins by hiding our eyes in shame when we were hurting as children, or resisting the love and adoration of guardians as we grow. It continues with running away as teenagers when someone asks questions or shows interest in our lives, being embarrassed when our parents brought us lunch in the school yard or deflecting when others swoon or compliment us.

Where did it all begin? Why have we built so many obstacles to love? I know in my case it all started with hurt. First with subtle comments that made me feel restricted, then bullying that made me feel worthless and unlovable, and so with every experience I created another shield, so many that at one time I felt incapable of being able to receive or feel love. As soon as it came my way a force kicked up and it was rejected. And to even begin to put down those shields meant I would be vulnerable to pain and suffering.

But what I learned from experience was that the more shields I put up the heavier life got. And as I garnered the strength to pull them down one by one, and the tenacity to persevere without collecting more then, yes, some pain momentarily set in, but what was far more profound was that I began to feel what love felt like again. And I wanted that feeling more. And so I worked on, and still work on, identifying the shields that I carry that are obstacles to the very force that lifts us higher: love, sweet unconditional love.

Reflection: The Final Frontier

Unconditional love is probably one of the most difficult of all things to master, and the final frontier in living a radically authentic life. But why is it so difficult? Why is it so hard to love ourselves and others right where we're at. What's created our resistance to it? It seems that it's the great divide. It brings constant challenges in our own lives as well as in our relationships with others. We're conditioned to believe that we, or others, must show up a certain way in order to receive it. And with the ideology of that conditioning is the birth of war: war within and without, in our own minds, our families and our societal structures.

We create boundaries and borders both within ourselves, our families and our communities. Don't get me wrong, there is nothing wrong with healthy boundaries; however, these boundaries create a resistance to empathy and an indifference to anything outside of our conditioning. They keep us static in our growth both individually and collectively and create barriers to interpersonal communication and self-love.

Why?

Because in order for us to love ourselves there is a plethora of conditioned criteria we must meet and the same goes for others. But where did it come from? Who decided? And why the fuck can't we just free ourselves from it? What's the hold-up? What's going to happen if one day we just decide to tear down the walls we've built against love and embrace ourselves and others with loving kindness just as we are? To respect and celebrate our points of differences rather than use them as catalysts for inner and outer conflict. It seems like such an easy solution, with a ripple effect that creates the kind of peace that passeth understanding. But there's just one problem, and depending who it is or you are, or how susceptible to conditioning you are, or your level of self-awareness, it could turn out to be the conflict of a lifetime. And that's your conditioning. A collective of your thoughts about who you and others are. Perception versus reality.

You see, if we can love one another without conditions, and in spite of our differences; politically, religiously and ideologically. If we can put down our armour, drop our shields and build on our strengths both individually and collectively. If we can stop 'shoulding' on ourselves and others. Let go of the conditioning we have that everything and everyone must show up the same to be valued or loved, beginning with ourselves, and it always begins with ourselves because when we have the ability to love ourselves without conditions, we have the ability to love others just the same. No matter what. And we must remember that unconditional love is not without boundaries but without the conditions and bias that separate us from ourselves and others.

YOUR VIVID LIFE

This is it. There's no better time than now. You've heard the whispers – perhaps the screams – of a life trapped somewhere between conditioning and resistance. I've shared my personal stories in hope that you'll see yours. I've shared what works for me, and what doesn't, in hope of helping you find your way. Through solitude, awareness, worth and environment I have mirrored our conditioning; in connections, evolution, nourishment and play, the path of least resistance; and through service, gratitude, movement and unconditional love, the path to a radically authentic life.

It's your turn to take the wheel, to claim captain of your ship and shape your destiny with radical authenticity. Your life, your way. But only your way, in your time. The journey is yours, the path your choice. And each experience along the way your opportunity to bring you closer to the truth, your truth.

We share a collective humanity, but within it an individual quest. What's your quest? What's burning inside you to unveil? Only you know, and the rest of us wait patiently for you to shine. For your piece of the puzzle of the universe to fit perfectly with ours. Wholeness collectively and individually is the path to peace. And through our own self-inquiry we find the wisdom we need to take the journey.

Every experience has been an opportunity to birth our truest selves. Do you hear the calling? When watching the memorial of our greatest men and women, you feel their heart with yours. When listening to the greatest who ever spoke, you hear your voice within theirs. When experiencing the voice of earth angels sing with all their soul, you feel it in yours. You're being called to greatness. Because that's what you are. Greatness manifests as the fingers of the universe, here, participating in this earth school, and all with all its yin and yang, ebb and flow, find the stillness there to be reminded of who you are.

Whether it's barefoot in the woods, meditating in the red rocks of Sedona, on your knees before your creator, a heart to heart with a friend, a Thanksgiving dinner, writing your journal, in Downward Dog, or looking through the eyes of another. Wherever you go, there you are. Your voice, your destiny waiting to be birthed. Calling you home to, as Gary Zukav calls it, 'The Seat of the Soul', or as it's referred to by Caroline Myss, your 'Sacred Contract'.

But only you know what's within it, and only if you get still enough to listen. But not if you're distracted by the collective voice of the world. Not if you're allowing resistance, masked as many things, with many faces, to pull your strings. No, No. Only if you have the courage to stop, look, and listen.

We've heard in it songs, read it in poetry, listened to it in churches, heard it spoken by great men and women, and watched it come alive in fairytales on screen and in theatres. 'Listen to your heart' and it calls you, it whispers to you in daydreams. Perhaps you're at the market, in class, or mid-conversation and something speaks to you. You stop, observe, right there is where it's at. That's the voice of your own heart calling you home to who you truly are, your radically authentic self. But then the silence dissipates, the noise of the world resumes, and then temporary amnesia sets in. You surrender to resistance, grab conditioning's hand and allow it to walk you through your life like a prisoner. And from time to time you'll hear its voice, and perhaps one day you'll heed its call, but not until you're ready. Not until you have the experience that creates the shift in awareness that ignites your soul with a light that can never be dimmed.

And there it is, that song again: 'This little light of mine' – such a simple childhood hymn but with such power. It instantly has the ability to cut through the darkest of days and remind me of who I am. But what reminds you? What words? What experiences? Perhaps there's a book, or a movie? Every time I watch *Eat Pray Love* I am reminded of my innate desire to live a passionate, spiritual life in deep connection with who I truly am. And I'm reminded that life, through all my experiences, whether volunteering in South Africa, horse and carriage in Ireland, fondue in Switzerland, or reading words through tears at my only sibling's funeral, is speaking to me, and through me offering its wisdom and encouraging me to speak my truth, even if my voice is shaking.

It takes immense courage to speak our truth. It's hard enough to hear it ourselves sometimes, but when we do, we give others permission to do the same. And the more in alignment with truth we are the more at peace we are individually and collectively. Our individual voices are like cells within the universe, each one with its purpose, but together they make a whole. And as the great Prime Minster of Canada (my home sweet home) Justin Trudeau says, we are 'strong not in spite of differences, but because of them'. To be different is not, despite what we may have been conditioned to think, a negative thing; it's a truth thing because it's who we are. Perhaps we share similarities with others, maybe socially, spirituality or politically, but even so, we are different and it's a noble act to recognize this, and to act with its conviction in everything we do.

Diversity is a strength. It liberates and leads us closer to the truth of who we are, and the truth, so we've been told, 'sets us free'. Free to be who we are, to love who we are, and to love others, just the way they are. Now doesn't that just feel like a breath of fresh air? Relax your shoulders. Open your heart. Why must we always be in conflict with others? Because who we are truly in conflict with is ourselves. And until we have the experience from which we embody the wisdom to birth this truth, we will suffer. And from my experience, it's not just in life's biggest experiences, but in the little. It's not just in the giant leaps, but the baby steps. Our opportunity to embody who we are is in every single experience, in every single moment, of every single day.

Your life is speaking. And it's time that you listen up. From the beginning of time we have had the answer right at our fingertips, within every culture, every religion, every spiritual practice. It's been written and it's been spoken, 'Be Still and Know' that 'I am', 'we are'. And this is your opportunity. You can either file this book with the rest, or you can go back through each chapter and listen. Read the stories, breathe in their wisdom, skim the practices and find your voice amongst it all. Find your who, what, where, when, why and how within each section and birth that with conviction. Pick up a pen and begin to write your own Vivid Life.

What does your Vivid Life look like? What does it feel like to be living a Vivid Life every single day? It's time to take a road trip through your mind, through your life, and through every category in this book to have a closer look at where you are at, who you are with, and where you want to be.

Begin with your own custom solitude practice, an inner search, alone without distractions bearing witness to your thoughts and emotions, and listen. Build your awareness through taking inventory of your current condition and the experiences that moulded you. Dismantle the conditioning that has held you hostage, dictated your worth, and kept you a puppet. Clean your house – dust the corners of your life both mentally and physically. Polish the mirror, pay attention to what's in its reflection and then take action, surrounding yourself with the things and relationships that are in alignment with your intention, or highest good.

Work every day at your own personal evolution and don't allow yourself to stay static or step back into the patterns that kept you hostage. Consistently put yourself in the path that nourishes your own personal evolution whether through writing, books, programs, travel or the people you surround yourself with. Be mindful of what you put in your body, because what you put in is equal to what you get out. Healthy body, healthy mind, healthy spirit.

And remember to make it playful. We are immersed in sedentary lives that lack a sense of playfulness. Engaging in active play helps us break through resistance, releases negative energy and helps us come closer to our truest selves and desires. And through those desires find out more about who you are, what makes you different and then give that authenticity to the world with all you've got, aligning your desires to meet a service to humanity. And remember, if you have the strength, to have gratitude for all things, because all things have led you to where you are today and from this place you have the opportunity to choose a greater path, a higher vibration, one that is deeply in alignment with who you really are.

And with that understanding you must participate relentlessly in the manifestation of your desires. Take action, moving physically and mentally. Moving your body through walking, Yoga, jogging (whatever body movement that you truly desire and enjoy, not the latest trend just because everyone else is doing it) as well as taking action mentally by stepping in the direction of your desires, taking risks and having tenacity. Whether you're at 100% or not, it will work out. You're exactly where you're meant to be to get where you're going. Just don't sit there and think about it, get up and act – baby steps. Your movement is crucial to both mental and physical health. And don't be afraid to make mistakes, they're part of the process, and as Wayne Dyer said, 'if you stumble make it part of the dance'. The dance of life. Because whether you're a good dancer or not, nothing you do will disappoint me. Me, the me that is within you, the whisper, the voice, the connection between you and everything, that loves you, without conditions.

WATKINS

Sharing Wisdom Since 1893

The story of Watkins began in 1893, when scholar of esotericism John Watkins founded our bookshop, inspired by the lament of his friend and teacher Madame Blavatsky that there was nowhere in London to buy books on mysticism, occultism or metaphysics. That moment marked the birth of Watkins, soon to become the publisher of many of the leading lights of spiritual literature, including Carl Jung, Rudolf Steiner, Alice Bailey and Chögyam Trungpa.

Today, the passion at Watkins Publishing for vigorous questioning is still resolute. Our stimulating and groundbreaking list ranges from ancient traditions and complementary medicine to the latest ideas about personal development, holistic wellbeing and consciousness exploration. We remain at the cutting edge, committed to publishing books that change lives.

DISCOVER MORE AT:

www.watkinspublishing.com

Read our blog

Watch and listen to
our authors in action

Sign up to
our mailing list

We celebrate conscious, passionate, wise and happy living.
Be part of that community by visiting

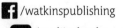 /watkinspublishing   @watkinswisdom
/watkinsbooks   @watkinswisdom